SUPERFANS

SUPERFANS

POWER, TECHNOLOGY, AND
MONEY IN THE MUSIC INDUSTRY

EMILY GUMBULEVICH

NEW DEGREE PRESS

COPYRIGHT © 2020 EMILY GUMBULEVICH

All rights reserved.

SUPERFANS

Power, Technology, and Money in the Music Industry

ISBN	978-1-64137-489-7	*Paperback*
	978-1-64137-490-3	*Kindle Ebook*
	978-1-64137-491-0	*Ebook*

Dedication

To my Pandemic Legacy partner: there's no one I would rather be with at the end of the world.

CONTENTS

	ACKNOWLEDGMENTS	9
	INTRODUCTION	13
	PART ONE	**23**
CHAPTER 1.	STARVING ARTISTS	25
CHAPTER 2.	HOW DID WE GET HERE?	39
CHAPTER 3.	PIRATES	57
CHAPTER 4.	WELL-OILED MACHINE	69
CHAPTER 5.	BEHIND THE VELVET CURTAINS	83
	PART TWO	**97**
CHAPTER 6.	MONEY	99
CHAPTER 7.	WHY NOW?	121
CHAPTER 8.	CHANGE	131
	CONCLUSION	149
	APPENDIX	157

ACKNOWLEDGMENTS

I would not have been set down the path of trying to help creators quit their day jobs without the courage to engage with artists at small live shows. For that courage and education, I am grateful for my longtime friend and college classmate, **Sean O'Keefe**, who convinced me to abandon my plans to watch *Pitch Perfect* again and instead to leave my studio apartment that fateful night in May 2015.

Without Sean's encouragement, I would not have met **Connor, Emily, Mikaela, Jenn, Aly, Chelsea,** or **Becca,** all of whom changed my life by showing me how to be a superfan. A special thank you to all of these friends for sharing their stories with me for this project and for being supportive listeners when I became overtired or frustrated with writing.

Thank you to my family for supporting me throughout this book-writing process, particularly to my parents, **Kristina** and **Kenneth,** for always encouraging me to work hard and pursue my constant curiosity, and for instilling in me a love of music at a very young age; to my siblings, **Jennifer** and **Kenny,** fellow music superfans, for understanding and supporting me through thick and thin; and to my aunts, uncles, grandparents, and cousins, without whom this book would not be published: **Matt** and **Tamara, Bobby** and **Carly, Steve** and **Cheryl, Robert** and **Karen, Tiffany** and **JP, Linda** and **Jimmy, Rick** and **Sharon, Lauren** and **Ken, Tony** and **Karen.**

Thank you to all of my interviewees. Without you, I would not have pivoted my thesis into what it is today. Thank you for sharing your stories, advice, and support of my mission to help creators find success.

Thank you to my educators, especially **Brian Pinaire,** for believing in me and pushing me to write. Thank you to Lehigh University for creating a wonderful atmosphere for creativity and curiosity to flourish, and for introducing me to some of the most amazing lifelong friends: **Victoria, Doug, Eric, Seth,** and **Carl.**

A very special thank you to **Eric Koester**—I appreciate your unwavering positivity and determination, and your dedication to your students.

Thank you to my editors, **Ashley** and **Bailee**, and to the New Degree Press team—**Brian, Leila, Amanda**—for your input, feedback, and most of all, patience throughout this process. You truly made this book transform from a collection of thoughts swirling around in my head into something that makes sense.

Thank you to my work colleagues, past and present, particularly to **Deborah, Simone, Tracy, Will, Kenny, Stacy,**

Randy, Katie, Sunish, Matthew, and **Andrew**, who helped me cross the finish line in my fundraising campaign, and to those who were patient with me when I came in with bags under my eyes or used my lunch hour to conduct interviews. I am lucky to have colleagues who support having passions outside of work.

Finally, a HUGE thank you to everyone who supported my book through my fundraising campaign and contributed ideas in my beta reader group. Without you, I would not have been able to complete this journey to seeing this book on shelves. I am so grateful for your support:

Angelo DeRosa
Kristen Sweeney
Matthew Diamond
Derek Clark
Nifemi Aluko
Matt Brooks
Shelley Strong
Linda Gottlieb

INTRODUCTION

"Forty years ago, co-writing a song with Ringo Starr would have provided me a house and a pool. Now, estimating a hundred thousand plays on Spotify, we guessed we'd split about eighty dollars,"[1] explains world-renowned composer, songwriter, and musician Van Dyke Parks.

In a 2014 op-ed, Parks describes heading up to Ringo Starr's home and spending two straight days working on a song together.[2] For the sake of argument, let's say that they each spent two typical workdays—eight hours per day—on the song. Splitting the aforementioned eighty dollars, which Parks later describes as "optimistic"[3] because Spotify typically pays a fraction of a cent per play, would result in a payment of forty dollars each for sixteen hours of work, or

---

1 "Van Dyke Parks on How Songwriters Are Getting Screwed in the Digital Age," Daily Beast, updated July 12, 2017.
2 Ibid.
3 Ibid.

$2.50 per hour. For comparison, US federal minimum wage in 2014 was $7.25/hour.[4]

Songwriters are not usually paid by the hour, though that might be more lucrative than how they typically get paid. Sometimes, they don't get paid at all. When it is deemed difficult to trace a song back to its copyright owners, royalties end up in what the industry has termed a "black box."[5] The royalties never reach the owners of the copyright so the streaming services, or whoever is attempting to pay the royalties, can keep the owed money indefinitely.

Further, the US Copyright Office allowed for bulk-filing of the necessary forms to claim that the owner of the copyright was too difficult to discern or find, which gave streaming services an easy out from having to find the rights' owners.[6] These services would file thousands of claims at once to avoid having to search for the rights holders to pay when songs from their catalogs were streamed.

---

4   "Changes in Basic Minimum Wages in Non-Farm Employment Under State Law: Selected Years 1968 to 2019," Wage and Hour Division, U.S. Department of Labor, revised January 2020.

5   "Fair Music: Transparency and Payment Flows in the Music Industry," Rethink Music, Berklee Institute for Creative Entrepreneurship, July 14, 2015.

6   Larry Miller, "How Music Got Modernized," October 24, 2018, in *Musonomics*, SoundCloud, podcast, MP3 audio, 10:54.

BLACK BOX

Van Dyke Parks' story is just one small example of how broken the music industry is today, and unfortunately, this is not a new problem. In 1781, a newspaper declared that "the music-shop keepers take the money, and for the composer remains only the honour, by which he is to live."[7]

I always imagined that behind the big velvety red curtains in every old theatre worldwide, there hummed a well-oiled machine: the music industry. I thought that the industry had plans for every artist to follow in order to make it big: a clear path to fame, big fat checks, and private jets.

I was dead wrong. My Disney-esque image of the music industry, rooted in *The Lizzie McGuire Movie* and *Josie and the Pussycat Dolls* ignorance, slowly broke down over the past five years as I educated myself:

- A major milestone of success for creators is being able to quit their day jobs and live off of the money they make from music. Sometimes it takes years to reach this milestone.
- The industry isn't just confusing and opaque for fans—it is for creators as well (artists, songwriters, musicians, producers, et al.).
- My ticket/merchandise/whatever money typically reaches the artist last.
- It is challenging to support yourself or your family with a career in music.

---

[7] David Hunter, "Music Copyright in Britain to 1800," *Music & Letters* 67, no. 3 (1986): 275.

- If we don't fix this, we risk losing an important part of our culture.

The term "black box"[8] is a great way to describe the current music industry in general. At the very least, there is a lack of transparency in how (and how much) people are paid, where fans' money ends up, and how to succeed. Contrary to other career paths, being an artist does not have a straight-line trajectory or clear next steps. In addition to weaving and bobbing, there are mountains and vales—times when artists seem to be "making it" and times when they are not able to feed themselves.

STARVING ARTIST

If we ignore this problem, we risk significant damage to our culture. Making music must be a choice that can support creators and their families or people will stop choosing it as a career. "If recording music cannot pay money, it will cease to become an occupation, it will become a hobby,"[9] proclaimed Alex Ebert, singer/songwriter of Edward Sharpe and the Magnetic Zeros, at Boston-based Berklee College of Music's Rethink Music event.

Further, X Ambassadors' manager Seth Kallen aptly notes, "If the artists can't feed themselves, there will be no more music."[10]

---

8   "Fair Music," Berklee, July 14, 2015.
9   "Rethink Music Fair Music Workshop," Rethink Music at Berklee College of Music, October 2, 2015, video, 00:34.
10 "Seth Kallen," Wisdom: A Portrait Series, The Manifesto, last accessed January 27, 2020.

A deeper look at the music industry over three hundred years from George Frederic Handel's first copyright in 1720 to Taylor Swift's battle with Scooter Braun in 2020 reveals that fans, artists, and inventors have taken the industry head-on when the longevity of culture is threatened. In the past, how the industry reacted to and bent with changes in laws, technology, and popular tastes would shape the following era of how people consume music.

We are fast approaching one of those times again. Since the rise of Napster and peer-to-peer file-sharing networks in 1999, earning a living off of recorded music has been even more difficult, pushing artists to rely more heavily on tour and synchronization (sync) revenues. Despite the inability to completely replace the recording revenues formerly generated from traditional music purchases, streaming services have changed how people find, listen to, and pay for music.

The availability of music via the internet and the rise in touring means fans are consuming more music than ever before in history.[11] In a recent episode of his podcast *Musonomics*, Larry Miller, a professor at New York University, discusses the 2019 International Federation of the Phonographic Industry's annual report on global music listening. Professor Miller reveals that "music listening is up a bit from 2018 with respondents typically spending eighteen hours a week listening to music"[12] and that "64 percent of all respondents

---

11 Larry Miller, "Mind the (Value) Gap," October 18, 2019, in *Musonomics*, SoundCloud, podcast, MP3 audio, 00:28.

12 Ibid.

access[ed] a music streaming service in the past month, up by about 7 percent over 2018."[13]

Furthermore, the increase in touring and the pervasiveness of social media have created deeper connections between artists and fans than ever before, leading to potential new levels of cooperation between creator and consumer.

A new music industry was born in the late 1990s to early 2000s from the adoption of services such as Napster and eventually Spotify, but key aspects, such as record labels and copyright laws, have not changed quickly enough in turn.

CHOCOLATE CHIP COOKIES

My understanding of success in the music industry began to fall apart in the summer of 2015. It all started unexpectedly… with a cookie.

X Ambassadors' drummer, Adam Levin, rummaged around in the back of his band's van and re-emerged with a translucent green rectangular Tupperware container. "You want a cookie?" he asked, as he pulled the lid off the container full of what looked like homemade chocolate chip cookies and extended it toward me.

It was after two in the morning on a Thursday and I had to be at the office in just a few hours, but I waited to meet X Ambassadors after their show at The Independent in San Francisco.

---

13   Miller, "Mind the (Value) Gap," 00:56.

Watching them pack up their equipment themselves and drive away in a cramped van, I felt my starstruck feeling wane as I realized that the band that I thought was wildly successful wasn't experiencing success according to what I had always envisioned. Where was the private jet? The bottles of Dom Perignon? The designer clothes?

As I waited, leaning against the stone exterior of the venue, nervous to meet this "famous" band, I was not expecting them to be loading up a black, beat-up, twelve-passenger van. I certainly didn't think lead vocalist and frontman, Sam Harris, would be driving it away wearing a black beanie cap and an all-black sweats ensemble, including a sweatshirt with *New York* across the chest that resembled something sold at an I-95 rest stop.

When I saw X Ambassadors drive away in their tour van in San Francisco in 2015, it was their *sixth* year playing together as a band.[14] They had already been signed by KIDinaKORNER/Interscope Records,[15] they had a manager,[16] and they had been discovered by another major artist (Dan Reynolds from Imagine Dragons).[17] They were not what I had originally thought of when I pictured the concept of "starving artists."

---

14 "X Ambassadors," Wikipedia, last accessed January 27, 2020.
15 "Creators," KIDinaKORNER Records, last accessed January 27, 2020.
16 "Homepage," This Fiction Management, last accessed January 27, 2020.
17 Danny Ross, "How to Manage Pop Stars Like X Ambassadors," *Forbes*, February 8, 2018.

So why were they driving themselves from gig to gig in the back of a crowded twelve-passenger Ford in the middle of the night? It didn't add up.

GATEKEEPERS

In the summer of 2015, my friends and I were seeing multiple live shows per week. We stayed up past midnight on Thursdays to be the first to hear what dropped on "New Music Friday," and we bought merchandise at every show. We were not typical fans—**we were "superfans."**

Despite all of our knowledge about the bands and their members, histories, and catalogs, when I brought up my concerns about X Ambassadors to my superfan friends, we had no idea what we could do to support the band more directly or why they hadn't hit private-jet-level success yet. It was clear that we had no idea what was going on inside of the music industry's black box.

When I started researching for this book, I hoped to find a formula for success for artists that operated *within* the well-oiled machine of the industry. I thought that the solution to this problem could be figured out by analyzing patterns and data. I hoped I would uncover something that others had missed.

Initially, I figured that critics or other industry players were the gatekeepers to success. These old gatekeepers used to hold the keys to production. Due to changes in society and technology, that is no longer true: savvy, scrappy creators can find ways around these industry actors to do most of the work themselves. Some of these old music industry gatekeepers still have influence and power, and some serve a real purpose in helping creators by taking care of non-artistic things like finances.

I was wrong about the existence of a moonshot formula for success in the data, but even though I failed to find it, one thing became clear from my research: the artist's road to success is paved by his/her music **superfans**.

PIVOTAL POINTS

We are fast approaching another pivotal point of change in history akin to that of Napster in the late 1990s and Spotify in the early 2010s.

In this book, I provide a high-level look at ways the music industry has changed in recent years. I explore the environment of the current music industry and how it came to be—breaking down the problems that are pushing creators, fans, and industry folks to bring about change today. I propose ways that fans, artists, entrepreneurs, and industry actors can collaborate to build a better music industry.

I wrote this book primarily for fans like me who want to better understand how the industry works today. My goal is to educate fans about where their concert ticket or Spotify subscription money ends up and how challenging it is to be a creator in today's world. I believe that fans have the most power in the industry as the customer is always at the center of everything. Fans can bring about change in how the industry treats creators.

This book is full of stories, insights, and lessons from experts in the field including:

- How Taylor Swift has built an unwaveringly loyal fanbase that has helped her through the ups and downs of her career.
- How Dave Matthews Band fans wielded the power of the internet to share unreleased songs.
- Chance the Rapper's success without the support of a label.
- Interviews of successful people in the music industry, such as the marketing manager for Live Nation in Philadelphia and the manager for X Ambassadors.

As I uncovered in my research and interviews, the music industry is a tightly locked black box. Some people stand to make a lot of money if artists are successful, but oftentimes, creators are the last ones paid…if they get paid at all.

In 1999, a would-be college dropout at Northeastern University changed the entire music recording business in a matter of months with Napster. In the early 2010s, Spotify changed how consumers access, find, interact with, and pay for music.

We are again at a tipping point in which fans have more power than they know. If harnessed properly, this superfan power will shape the future of the industry, for the better.

PART ONE

CHAPTER 1

STARVING ARTISTS

"You want a cookie?" Adam asked, as he pulled the lid off of a large rectangular Tupperware container and extended it toward me. Just moments before, X Ambassadors' drummer, Adam Levin, was rummaging around in the back of his band's van. He re-emerged with the translucent green plastic container full of homemade chocolate chip cookies that now appeared in front of me.

YOU ROCK

By the summer of 2015, I was seeing live music multiple times per week. I had spent the previous six months settling into Boston during its famous "Snowmageddon"[18] after moving from Washington, DC. I finally found a local group of friends as passionate about music as I am. They introduced me to the Boston live music scene, through which I began meeting bands after shows and building relationships with industry folks.

---

18 Erin Kayata, "Last Winter's Snowmageddon, by the numbers," *The Boston Globe*, November 8, 2015.

In late-July of that summer, I saw X Ambassadors open for Milky Chance at the House of Blues in Boston, which I considered to be a big deal for them since it's a legendary venue.[19] Around this time, I naively thought X Ambassadors had "made it" big.

Less than a week later, while in San Francisco for work, I discovered X Ambassadors had sold out a headlining show coming up at The Independent. I had been playing their new album *VHS* on repeat since it came out, but it was even better live. I bought a last-minute ticket off StubHub for three times the face value. I hoped the Independent would provide a more intimate experience than the House of Blues given its smaller size and different layout—and I couldn't get enough of *VHS*.

Since X Ambassadors was my friend Connor's favorite band and the show was on his birthday, I grabbed a card with a picture of a drum kit on the front that said *You Rock* on the inside on my way to the show. Upon arrival, I camped out in the first row of the general admission crowd against the stage during the openers so that I would have a prime spot for the entire X Ambassadors set and a shot at grabbing the setlist at the end—a lesson I learned from my new concert-going friends.

The band blew me away with an amazing show once again. I played the clarinet and sang in school groups growing up, so

---

[19] Matt Brooks of Sofar Sounds explained to me in our interview that artists dream of playing The House of Blues Boston because it was the first House of Blues venue and is one of the larger ones in the country.

I am always impressed to see Sam Harris playing the saxophone, singing, and dancing on stage without missing a beat. It is so much breathing, saliva, and stepping to coordinate all at once, and I know I couldn't do it.

After the show ended and the lights came up, the crowd cleared, and the staff began sweeping away the mess of trampled beer cans that littered the floor. Security quickly kicked me and the other stragglers out to the curb, but I was determined. I waited, leaning against the stone exterior walls of the venue in a short line of like-minded fans, despite the pleas of the venue staff to "just go home," my iPhone dying, and time ticking away into the early morning on a weekday.

The band finally appeared through the front door, equipment in arms, loading up their black, beat-up twelve-passenger van, appearing dead tired but elated to see fans. They took the time to talk to each of us, snap pictures, and even signed my friend's birthday card. Adam offered me a cookie and then soon enough, it was all over. They piled into their van and drove off into the night.

REALITY CHECK
I started back toward my Airbnb, starstruck from meeting one of my favorite bands that was on stage just moments before, taking in the dewy warm San Francisco air and reviewing the set in my mind.

I quickly snapped out of my trance when X Ambassadors drove up beside me at a stop sign. While they were stopped at the corner, I could hear a muffled discussion from their open windows about where to turn next. From what I could tell, lead vocalist and frontman, Sam Harris, was driving. I wondered how they fit all of their equipment and four bandmates into such a small vehicle, imagining sort of a game of Tetris happening in order to fit Adam and his drums.

I realized that the band I considered wildly talented and successful was now driving a crappy van past two in the morning after unloading and loading their own equipment. I couldn't help but wonder why and what it meant.

When I started to search for the answers, I found that:

- Creators are typically the last ones paid.
- Touring is hard but necessary in today's economy.
- The music industry is difficult to navigate due to a lack of transparency and a complex web of actors with competing interests.
- Creators struggle to make ends meet.

So, what does success look like for creators? Only three minutes into my half-hour interview with Katie Marshall, vocalist and half of the Brooklyn-based brother-sister pop duo, Paperwhite, I sprung that tough question on her, "What does success look like for you?"

"Success is a confusing word," Katie answered quickly.

She put it perfectly. Katie's answer adequately reflected the facial expressions, voice fluctuations, and hesitations that I received from every artist, fan, and industry professional that I have asked over the past few years. Success is difficult to define and differs depending on the artist you ask or the stage of his/her career.

However, for most creators, a common first milestone in success is the ability to quit their non-music day job, even if it means taking up side hustles here and there. It typically takes years to achieve.

For example, though singer-songwriter and flute-toting performing artist Lizzo has risen to the top of the charts quickly in recent years, she is no newcomer to the industry. In an impassioned Twitter post, responding to comments that she was an overnight success story, she made it clear to followers how long she worked to make it to the top:

8 years of touring, giving out free tix to my undersold shows, sleepless nights in my car, losing my dad & giving up on music, playing shows for free beer & food with -32$ in my bank account, constantly writing songs, hearing "no" but always saying "yes"

Glad I never gave up. (@lizzo, November 25, 2019)[20]

It is important for fans to understand and appreciate artists' challenging journeys, like Lizzo's, because they have the power to help these hardworking artists find success.

---

20 Lizzo, "8 years of touring, giving out free tix to my undersold shows, sleepless nights in my car, losing my dad & giving up on music, playing shows for free beer...," Twitter, November 25, 2019, 1:29 a.m.

This milestone is particularly important in the story of fans and artists cooperating to influence the future of the music industry. The flow of money from fan to creator must be more direct in order for new artists to hit this key point in their careers earlier and more often. This change in how artists are paid is vital to preserving the influx of new music and the continuation of art.

Fans are at the core of this change because they are the consumers of music—pumping money into the industry. If fans were to trace where their money goes, they would find that a lot of it does not end up in the pockets of their favorite bands. Furthermore, consumer behaviors have changed since the early 2000s because fans are generally spending less money on recorded music but more money on live music. In this way, "the way artists earn most of their money differs dramatically from the way most fans enjoy the music artists create."[21]

In the past, consumers would purchase physical recordings of their favorite music, such as on a compact disc (CD), from the local music store. With the rise of the internet and rapidly changing technology, the CD became obsolete very quickly and was replaced by digital copies of music called mp3s. Though there are ways to legally obtain and consume mp3s by purchasing streaming subscriptions or digital downloads of music from an online store, as of the 2019 IFPI annual report on global music listening that Professor Miller discusses in Musonomics, "27 percent of those surveyed used

---

21 Alan B. Krueger, *Rockonomics: A Backstage Tour of What the Music Industry Can Teach Us About Economics and Life* (New York: Penguin Random House, 2019), 10.

unlicensed methods to listen to or obtain music in the past month,"[22] revealing that piracy of music is still very much an issue. Lack of revenue from recording royalties directly impacts creators' abilities to quit their day jobs.

LUNCH HOUR
I am a huge Paperwhite fan. I first met Katie and her brother Ben in 2016 when they opened for Great Good Fine Ok at Brighton Music Hall in Allston, Massachusetts. They were hanging out at the back of the venue by the merchandise tables. I distinctly recall how humble and kind they were despite playing a bop of a show.

When Katie agreed to an interview, I was elated. I couldn't wait to ask her about her career, the band, and when fans would hear new music.

Sitting in a conference room in the back corner of my tech start-up's office during my typically nonexistent "lunch hour," I tried to scarf down my Sweetgreen Kale Caesar while on mute in between questions, thankful for the lack of video feed on our call. I asked Katie to elaborate on why success was so confusing. I'd forgotten how different her voice sounded when she was talking versus singing.

Her humility shined through as she admitted to me with ease, "I do feel grateful that I have been able to do music, but it's not like it has necessarily been easy. I would like to feel more comfortable."

---

22 Miller, "Mind the (Value) Gap," 1:10.

Her answer didn't surprise me. Rather, it sounded eerily similar to the ones I had heard before when meeting bands at the back of music halls. Despite my familiarity with this reality, my heart still crept into my throat as I felt overcome with sadness and confusion. I appreciated her art and wanted to make sure that she and her brother could keep creating, comfortably.

Artists are struggling to support themselves on music alone. Katie Marshall has hit the point in her career at which she can mostly live off of her music but it's not as glamorous as we might think—she still picks up short-term odd jobs outside of music for extra money, like babysitting, producing floral arrangements, or food styling.

It is challenging to make it through the non-touring months when expenses are high due to studio fees and other costs related to recording new music, revenues are low due to a lack of gigs and the staleness of the past album release, and time is minimal because of the work required to produce a new album. "You could write music for a full year so you're not touring and you're not releasing…you're not really making money," she explained.

So, where does the money go?

MONEY

Given today's economy, it should not be surprising that it has not been easy for creators like Katie Marshall of Paperwhite to make enough money to stay afloat from music alone.

Bootlegging and music piracy existed before the internet, but the internet made it easier and more pervasive. Beginning in 1999, the average consumer began downloading recorded music for free in bulk via online peer-to-peer networks like Napster. Recording industry revenues have fallen sharply since the shift in consumer behavior away from paying for recorded music.

In the United States, in particular, one of the largest music markets in the world:

- 1999 was the peak for recorded music sales at $14.6 billion.[23]
- After a sharp decline in revenue from 2000 through 2010, levels flattened out at around $7 billion for the next five years.[24]
- With the rise of streaming, the industry began to see recovery after 2015.[25]
- In 2018, RIAA reported nearly $10 billion in sales,[26] approximately 68 percent of peak.
- In 1999, Compact Discs (CDs) accounted for 87.9 percent[27] of all revenue, but in 2018, that share dropped to 7.1 percent[28]—this makes sense since the computer I'm

---

23 "US Recorded Music Revenues by Format," US Sales Database, Recording Industry Association of America (RIAA), last accessed January 27, 2020.
24 Ibid.
25 Ibid.
26 Ibid.
27 Ibid.
28 Ibid.

using to write this book on doesn't even have a CD-ROM drive.

The rise to $14.6 billion in sales in 1999 was unprecedented.[29] Just ten years before Napster, the industry reported only $6.6 billion in sales.[30] Compact discs helped the music industry generate the most sales it had ever seen and then quickly, the internet made it all come crashing down.

QUIT YOUR DAY JOB
The goal of this book is to bring about changes in consumer behavior that ultimately help creators quit their day jobs.

My book analyzes changes in the music industry due to technology and shifts in consumer behavior since the adoption of Napster in 1999. I postulate that we are going through a similar shift today, perhaps not as large but certainly as important, due to the increase in transparency between creator and consumer about how the industry works. With the rise of ethical consumption in every other part of our lives—food, alcohol, clothing, etc. —now is a perfect time for fans to open the black box of the industry and demand fair pay for creators. Simultaneously, fans need to understand the damaging impact of illegal downloading on the livelihoods of creators. Finally, entrepreneurs and old industry giants need to cooperate to build rules of operation that work with the new way that fans consume music through technology.

---

29 Ibid.
30 Ibid.

Despite all of the other definitions of success, each highly personalized to the artist or professional, the milestone or benchmark I heard mentioned in nearly every interview I conducted or article I read was the concept of being able to support oneself on music alone.

This milestone is important for a few reasons:

1. It means that art is the musician's full-time career,
2. It enables the artist to make more art, and
3. It empowers the artist to focus on achieving artistic milestones because the need to meet basic needs is no longer a dark cloud looming overhead.

Katie Marshall summed it up well when she explained to me that "success feels like I'm able to do music. I'm able to have that be the day-to-day and my full career. I'm able to live the life I want and be able to create music every day."

Fans and creators can collaborate to change the industry in order to make it easier for creators to live off of their work. Now is the time for this change to happen.

FOLLOWING A DREAM
I became personally invested in helping musicians achieve success because I know firsthand what it is like to work extra jobs to make ends meet in the pursuit of a dream. My dream was much easier to attain and considerably more reliable once I got there, but nevertheless, I can empathize with creators like Katie Marshall who are pursuing their passions.

The day after I graduated from college, I packed up everything I owned in an assortment of trash bags and old neon-colored Adidas gym bags. I drove my old, dinged-up silver Honda Civic four hours southeast to Washington, DC, where I had nowhere to live and a part-time gig as a barista at Starbucks. Back then, it was my dream to live in a city and work for the US government, so I did whatever it took to make that a reality.

I saw room after room from the Craigslist roommate postings, including one in a house where the toilets didn't flush properly so a large trash can next to a pedestal sink overflowed with used toilet paper—a sight and a smell I'll unfortunately never forget. After landing a contractor job at the Securities and Exchange Commission, I finally rented an overpriced five-hundred-square-foot studio apartment in Arlington, Virginia. It was next door to the scene of a recent homicide. My parents were thrilled.

At one point, my side hustle wasn't cutting it, so I had to sell my car to make rent. I rode the bike that my parents bought me for my thirteenth birthday four miles each way down a poorly lit bike path to and from Starbucks in my all-black barista uniform. I'll never forget the nights that it rained and the cold water stung my face, or when we couldn't close the store quickly enough so I would end up leaving past 11:00 p.m., anxiety and fear pumping adrenaline through my veins enough to push me home at record speeds. Again, my parents were thrilled—but at least I wore a helmet?

I never could afford a bed frame to get my thin IKEA foam mattress off the floor. I lived off the microwavable vegetable medleys that the local Target sold in the frozen "meals for one" aisle. I knew very few people in the area because I spent so much time at work.

It was hard, but it felt worth it because I was following my dream.

DOUBLE SHIFT

Thankfully, my double-shift life was short-lived, but that's not the case for most musicians. The music industry has not adapted to changes in technology and consumer behavior in order to ensure that creators are still paid fairly. There are so many fingers in the creators' metaphorical pie, and it is very challenging to see where fans' money ends up. Further, the pie as a whole continues to transform as recording revenues in the music industry have drastically fallen since Napster, leading to a heavy reliance on touring income.

Though it has not always been as complicated, as far back as the 1700s, creators were seeking ways to get paid fairly for their art. George Frederic Handel made "the sarcastic remark that [his publisher] Walsh should write the next opera and that Handel should publish it."[31]

If there's no clear path to earning money by making music, musicians will never hit this important milestone of success.

---

31 Frank Kidson, "Handel's Publisher, John Walsh, His Successors, and Contemporaries," *The Musical Quarterly* 6, no. 3 (1920): 443.

CHAPTER 2

HOW DID WE GET HERE?

It was the spring of 2018. The strong Denver sun was setting over the mountains and the glare struck my face through a window in my small one-bedroom apartment as I sat on the edge of my gray IKEA couch on the phone with my long-time friend Chance Jennings. At this time, Chance managed his brother Tucker's band Call Security, having just recently made the huge change from investment banking in New York City to artist management in Providence, Rhode Island.

I always picture Chance as I knew him at eighteen: wearing a plaid flannel shirt and khaki cargo pants, with long, straight, unkempt hair. Since I could never really see Chance wearing a freshly pressed suit and sporting the typical investment banker-style slicked-back hair, presumably working on a double-digit floor of a skyrise on Wall Street, the switch to artist management reconciled the image of him in my mind.

I had been searching for the formula for success for nearly three years since seeing X Ambassadors drive off in their twelve-passenger van in San Francisco. I contacted Chance hoping to learn more about what he learned so far about the industry as an outsider breaking in.

Our call felt like it could last forever. I overflowed with questions. I learned so much, like how difficult it is to play shows outside of your hometown and how little streaming pays, but it was still unclear to me why the industry was so broken. Despite living through one of the most tumultuous times in history for the music recording industry, I didn't fully understand what had happened that brought us here.

The music industry that I assumed was a well-oiled machine seemed more like something rusty and dilapidated in the corner of a junkyard.

How did we get here?

This chapter is meant to serve as a brief overview of important concepts and music industry history, in order to set the scene for where we go from here. It is structured in three sections:

- CONNECTION: Music is an important part of our culture, as an expression of the human condition that we use to connect or communicate with one another.
- PROFITS: People in the industry other than creators try to profit off of music by revolutionizing technology to increase access to music.
- LAWS: As technology has advanced and revolutionized the way that fans consume music, the laws protecting the artists and industry operations have lagged behind.

CONNECTION

Just as we all really "feel" what she's saying when Lizzo sings "Truth Hurts," which is probably why it stuck around at number one on the Billboard Hot 100 Chart[32] for seven weeks, humans have been connecting over music for centuries.

Music is a way to share in various emotions and experiences as a part of human existence. All music, from hymns sung in cathedrals to top pop hits played on the radio, contributes to our culture in some way by communicating about a certain time in history or by being timeless expressions of commonalities among us. I saw this clearly when I caught up with a longtime friend, Simone Ellis, about her tastes in music.

I finished up a long day at my office across the street and was now sitting at a cozy corner table in the back of the dimly lit Marliave restaurant, one of the oldest chef-owned restaurants in Boston. Sitting kitty-corner from me was my old friend Simone, who also happens to be the daughter of the industry executive who helped the Jonas Brothers become giant pop stars by organizing their first mall tours.

It had been a few months since we had been able to get together due to our prohibitively busy schedules, and we caught up about our new apartments and recent promotions to management. We sipped craft cocktails with funny names like "Boston Tea Party" and shared a charcuterie board of French cheeses with spiced nuts, lavender honey, and fig jam accouterments.

---

32 "Hot 100 Chart," Billboard, last accessed January 27, 2020.

It didn't take much time for our conversation to turn to music. Simone knows that I rarely don't have plans to see a live show, so she asked me about the bands I'd seen recently. I told her that I shockingly had not been to any concerts in a few weeks since seeing one of my favorite bands, Great Good Fine Ok, on the Monday night after driving eight hours back from Firefly Music Festival in Delaware.

"I don't think I've ever been so exhausted in my life," I explained. "Seeing them three times in three days was worth it, though; I got a signed poster!" At this point, I have plenty of signed merchandise and set lists from Luke and Jon from Great Good Fine Ok. Simone knows that, so she was not surprised to hear that I was expanding my collection.

Still, she made a face indicating that she doesn't understand how or why I consume live music the way that I do, so I switched the conversation back to her to ask about her favorite musicians. Simone immediately began blushing. She hesitated and looked down at her half-eaten crostini, as if to ponder if she should take another bite in order to push off the question longer.

Even to me, one of her closest friends, she was nervous to admit to her fandom of the Jonas Brothers: "I'm lame. I've seen Nick Jonas in the Jonas Brothers when he was touring by himself, when he was touring with Demi Lovato," she explained, listing all of the times and ways she has seen Nick Jonas.

She lifted her head slowly to look up at me, brushing her straight dark hair away from her face, seemingly expecting to see or hear an admonishing reaction akin to when someone admits to loving Nickelback or Creed. I just nodded and asked her why she feels such a strong connection to the Jonas Brothers and Demi Lovato.

Relieved, she continued on to tell me more about her fandom: "I felt such a connection to Demi Lovato growing up. I just remember seeing her break down on stage a few times when she was singing really emotional songs."

Simone followed Demi Lovato through her career, from when the artist got her start on television at age ten to her present pop stardom. She watched as Demi struggled with various personal issues ranging from mental health to substance addiction and abuse, ultimately leading up to a drug overdose that nearly ended her life in July 2018.[33]

Though Simone has not personally had to deal with the same issues, she still felt connected to the singer in those experiences as they revealed how human Demi was, even as a pop star. Demi struggled with the same insecurities as many young women. "Being vulnerable on stage is a huge thing. I was sitting in the last possible row in the TD Garden and I still felt connected to her," Simone explained.

Music plays an important role in connecting us. Alan Krueger puts this well in his book about music and economics, *Rockonomics*: "[i]n a highly polarized age, music is one of the few endeavors in modern life that unites people from

---

33 Dana Point Rehab, "Demi Lovato Doing Well After Overdose and Drug Rehab," Dana Point Rehab Campus, October 22, 2018.

different political, religious, cultural, regional, ethnic, and racial backgrounds."[34]

A marketing manager for Live Nation, Becky Blumenthal, recounted a similar experience of feeling connected with others through music despite the distance from the stage or the crowd around her. She went to see one of her favorite bands, Snarky Puppy, play a free festival in Morocco. Becky waded into the sea of people to watch the show from the middle of the audience.

Becky recalled that even though she was surrounded by people from all over the world, standing in an audience representative of all of the different races, languages, beliefs, socioeconomic backgrounds, education levels, and more, she felt so comforted by the people of the audience: "On the outside, it seemed like I had nothing in common with the rest of the audience, but really, we were all there for the same reason—the music."

Snarky Puppy is a jazz band so there are typically no words, which means that their music is much more global in reach. As Becky described watching the jazz musicians on stage to me, I could feel the weight of this life-changing moment in her words. She explained that in jazz, "It's about the feelings and the way that the musicians are communicating with you without having to use the spoken language."

We can harness the powerful ways in which music connects us to each other in order to bring about the change we need to see in the industry.

---

34 Krueger, *Rockonomics*, 25.

PROFITS

As far back as the 1700s, technological advances have led to increased access to music but oftentimes have also led to ways for distributors of music to make more money off of music than the creators of the music themselves.

For example, the infamous music publisher John Walsh revolutionized music printing in England, and "[b]y the end of 1705, Walsh dominated England's music printing industry."[35] One key reason that Walsh rose to power was because he invented a more cost-effective, faster method of engraving the plates used for printing sheet music, which was the main way music was recorded and shared at this time in history.[36]

Much of Walsh's fortune (and that of his successor, his son) came from reprinting George Frederic Handel's works. Though he deserves credit for the many improvements he made to printing that led to both increased sales and greater profit margins, the product Walsh sold was ultimately not his own—he sold the creations of Handel. Yet, as evidenced by Handel's remark in chapter one, it was often more lucrative to be the publisher of the music than to be the creator: "[w]riting was not the way for an author or composer to make a living before the second half of the eighteenth century."[37]

---

35 Richard Hardie, "All Fairly Engraven?": Punches in England, 1695 to 1706," *Notes* 61, no. 3 (2005): 631.

36 David Hunter, "The Printing of Opera and Song Books in England, 1703-1726," *Notes* 46, no. 2 (1989): 329.

37 Hunter, "Music Copyright in Britain to 1800," 272.

As technology revolutionized the ways in which music is produced and consumed, the industry became more complex. With each of these added complexities in the music industry came another industry actor to take a piece of the pie, until eventually, the slices became tiny for everyone. By the 1990s, a somewhat popular performing artist would likely incur costs related to:

- a manager or management staff
- copyright and contract legal assistance
- a record label and recording (studio time, physical record costs)
- a music publisher
- one or more performance rights organization's (PRO) membership fees
- an event promoter
- a talent buyer and a booking agent for a live performance
- music video production
- marketing/press and public appearance staff

Depending on the contracts that the artist has negotiated, there is not much left for the artist—and that was the case when people still bought music outright.

In an episode of the *Musonomics* podcast run by Professor Larry Miller from New York University's Steinhardt School of Culture, Education, and Human Development, musician Miranda Mulholland told Professor Miller, "I started my career around 2000...so pretty much the worst time to ever get into music."[38] Miranda is, of course, referring to the

---

38 Miller, "Mind the (Value) Gap," 2:02.

fact that the early 2000s was a disruptive time for the music industry due to the proliferation of illegal file-sharing that led to the drop in recording revenues.

Even though streaming services such as Spotify, Pandora, and YouTube have increased the amount of music fans consume and have globalized music by improving access to music internationally, Miranda aptly points out that the product these platforms are selling is the platform itself. She describes music as "the window dressing for all these other companies to sell their product"[39] rather than the product itself, whereas to an artist like Miranda, *music* is the product.

In the past, when consumers purchased music in the form of digital downloads or compact discs, they were buying music as the core product. Yet even then, format played some role in the purchasing decision. Stephen Witt explains in his book *How Music Got Free* that despite the best efforts of lobbyists for the recording industry, the record companies themselves, and the technology giants like Phillips who pioneered the CD, music still "got free" in the early 2000s.[40]

Witt tells the story of a team of engineers led by Karlheinz Brandenburg at the Fraunhofer Institute in Germany who spent over a decade compressing music into small enough file sizes to be streamed over phone lines.[41] He explains that "the Moving Picture Experts Group (MPEG) —the standards

---

39 Miller, "Mind the (Value) Gap," 12:23.
40 Stephen Witt, *How Music Got Free: A Story of Obsession and Invention* (New York: Penguin Books, 2016).
41 Witt, *How Music Got Free*, 9.

committee that even today decides which technology makes it to the consumer marketplace—convened a contest in Stockholm"[42] which turned into a "format war."[43] Though Brandenburg's team's mp3 initially lost the contest to the mp2 format (the compact disc), it ultimately won with the proliferation of free software his team released to the public.[44]

Early internet hackers used this software to rip and share recorded music. Eventually, a college student at Northeastern created Napster, which shared the free music that had only previously been shared via secret hacker forums with everyday internet users. Witt explains that the record companies shut Napster down but could not stop the mp3 player from being created, thereby providing a path forward for the demise of purchased music as consumers had a way to listen to their bootlegged mp3 libraries on the go. In this way, the format mattered as much as the music, if not more.[45]

LAWS

The law is often behind advances in technology and not just when it relates to music. At one tech startup for which I worked, the motto was, "When you get sued, you know you've succeeded in disrupting the status quo with your product." A convenient example of this concept is the rise of Uber.

---

42 Witt, *How Music Got Free*, 17.
43 Witt, *How Music Got Free*, 21.
44 Witt, *How Music Got Free*, 98.
45 Witt, *How Music Got Free*, 97-98.

Washington, DC was the first big city I had ever lived in. The DC metro area is comprised of parts of Maryland and Virginia, with Washington, DC in the middle where most people in the area work. This cross-section of three states presented a real issue when it came to hailing a cab ride to or from outside of DC-proper. Different state and local laws governed taxi companies, which meant, for instance, that if I took a taxi home from my job near Union Station in DC-proper to my apartment in Arlington, Virginia, not only would it cost me an arm and a leg and take at least thirty minutes, but the cab driver would not be allowed to pick up a ride back from Virginia into the city.

Taxi drivers must have a rider in their cab at all times or they are just wasting gas, so it was difficult to convince any cab drivers in the city to drive into Virginia or Maryland, or vice versa, due to the lack of cab fare back to their locality. Uber recognized this problem and ultimately turned to the "black car" drivers (livery) who didn't have to abide by the same laws as those with the taxicab commission for a solution. The startup also realized that akin to taxi drivers, these drivers were not making money in between their regularly scheduled rides. Harnessing the power of mobile app technology, while operating in the gray areas of the laws at the time, Uber disrupted the taxi business in the DC area and was ultimately sued.

The lawsuits against Uber forced the local governments to reconsider their laws and adjust them to attempt to balance the playing field for taxis versus ride-sharing apps, but these law adjustments were too little too late. Uber and others had already changed the way consumers took taxis.

The same sort of thing has happened several times throughout the history of the music industry. Technology disrupts the status quo, shifting share from one side to another, until lawsuits follow and then changes in laws attempt to ensure fairness.

The music industry has many regulations and protections of rights in place to ensure that creators are paid fairly. However, these laws continue to fall short because they fail to keep up with changes in technology. Mitch Glazier, the president of the Recording Industry Association of America (RIAA), puts it well in his interview with Professor Larry Miller: "Congress enacts protections like a flashpoint in time for a particular technology because the advent of that technology creates a need to do something."[46]

Referring back to the example of John Walsh, another key part of the reason that he was able to amass such a fortune was that the copyright protections we know today did not truly exist in his time. Walsh was "the first to employ unauthorized publication as a standard practice,"[47] but "unauthorized publication in the sense of printing a composer's work without his approval was not illegal except in a few very limited circumstances."[48]

Eventually, the laws attempted to catch up, granting fourteen-year copyright protections against unauthorized reproductions of composers' works, but

---

46 Miller, "How Music Got Modernized," 17:03.
47 Hunter, "Music Copyright in Britain to 1800," 272.
48 Ibid.

Until 1774, remedy at common law was available against unauthorized printing, but as the grounds for such an action were uncertain, it is not surprising that no composer felt able to take on a publisher in the courts. The financial resources required would have been a sufficient deterrent.[49]

Even composers who had sold their works to publishers for legal reproduction, "often suffered the chagrin of seeing publishers grow rich,"[50] while they remained poor.

Many of the lawmakers in the US (and other major music markets) today are wrestling with the same questions as those first copyright laws in 1700s England:

- What is a fair market rate for music?
- What is fair use of a license to or copy of a music recording?
- How can the government ensure that technological innovation and the economy are not stifled whilst preserving the rights of intellectual property owners?
- How liable are the inventors of new technology that disrupts an economic status quo?

In October 2018, the United States Congress passed the latest of these legal protections for creators, the Orrin G. Hatch-Bob Goodlatte Music Modernization Act (MMA). I will explain the importance of the MMA in today's changing industry landscape later in chapter seven, but first, it is key to understand what led to this monumental legislation.

---

49 Hunter, "Music Copyright in Britain to 1800," 277.
50 Hunter, "Music Copyright in Britain to 1800," 275.

The United States has had some sort of legal protection for artistic creations since its inception. The first instance of language protecting artists' creations can be found in the US Constitution, in Article 1, Section 8, "The Congress shall have Power... To promote the Progress of Science and useful Arts, by securing for limited Times to Authors and Inventors the exclusive Right to their respective Writings and Discoveries."[51]

From there, as technology revolutionized the way that music is distributed and consumed around the world, copyright protections evolved, but these improvements to the laws were almost always too late due to the slow pace of compromise. The former general counsel for the National Music Publishers Association, Jacqueline Charlesworth, explained that negotiations around the 1976 Copyright Act "went on for twenty years"[52] before getting passed. She recounted that the head of the United States Copyright Office wittily said at the time of its passing that "Well, this is a great 1950s copyright act."[53]

Though the outdated 1976 Copyright Act and the 1998 Digital Millennium Copyright Act attempted to ensure that creators were paid fairly, these laws fell short. Two key aspects of these laws allowed for the rise of first—illegal downloading via peer-to-peer file-sharing networks such as Napster, and second—creation of online content streaming services with large music libraries:

---

51 "The Constitution of the United States: The Bill of Rights & All Amendments," last accessed on January 27, 2020.
52 Miller, "How Music Got Modernized," 7:30.
53 Miller, "How Music Got Modernized," 7:33.

- First, internet service providers were not held liable for the activities performed over their networks,[54] therefore allowing illegal downloading to become prolific without many consequences. This was made obvious with RIAA's unsuccessful lawsuits against internet service providers, such as Recording Industry Association of America v. Verizon Internet Services.[55]
- Second, the outdated copyright laws had a loophole of sorts whereby the streaming giants could bulk file forms claiming the lack of ability to find the true copyright owners, thereby giving them a pass from paying out royalties to those owners.[56] They even did this for popular and contemporary music for which the rights' owners should be easy to find, but it was only recently noticed.[57]

Given the immense advancement in technology since 1998 but complete lack of reform until the MMA in 2018, there was little recourse via the law to remediate the imbalance of power between the old and new industry actors.

Finally, despite outdated laws, the primary avenue for resolution of these conflicts has been via lawsuits. Though the big record labels tried to collaborate with Napster at the start, they ultimately could not reach an agreement and resorted

---

54 Miller, "Mind the (Value) Gap," 5:28.
55 Jason Krause, "BREAKING UP DOWNLOADING: Recording Industry Keeps Fighting Illegal File Sharing With Even More Lawsuits," *ABA Journal* 92, no. 4 (2006): 18.
56 Miller, "How Music Got Modernized," 10:54.
57 Ibid.

to expensive lawsuits instead.[58] As I will build upon later in chapter eight, I believe that industry actors need to adapt to the changes in technology by joining the technological revolution rather than fighting against it.

FROM ABBA TO ZZ TOP[59]

As a kid of the '90s, I watched my parents' brown plastic milk cartons of vinyl long-plays and cassette tapes turn into alphabetized floor-to-ceiling stacks of CD jewel cases.

Quickly, in addition to the commercial CDs we'd purchased at Strawberries, our collection of burned CD-RWs (short for Compact Disc Read-Write) began to grow: from my dad's famous 2001 Christmas mix that he still plays to this day to my 2003 thirteenth birthday party mix that I decorated with purple Sharpies.

I had access to all of the free music I could have ever wanted at my fingertips. Before services like Napster, LimeWire, and Kazaa were shut down, I had (illegally) built a hefty library on iTunes from ABBA to ZZ Top.[60]

I had so much music, in fact, that I needed to plug an external hard drive into my computer just to play a song from

---

58 Witt, *How Music Got Free*, 126.
59 Krueger, *Rockonomics*, 21.
    My iTunes library was actually from ABBA to ZZ Top, but it is worth mentioning that after writing this phrase, I found it written this way in Alan Krueger's *Rockonomics* as well.
60 Krueger, *Rockonomics*, 21. See above.

my iTunes library. During my freshman year at Lehigh University, I shared a room with a Marching 97 piccolo player, Julia, in McClintock-Marshall Hall. She once took a series of pictures of me trying to find the right song to play. The photos paint a scene that's quite comical but was actually a pretty accurate portrayal of me in college.

In them, I'm precariously seated on my raised twin XL bed with one leg hanging off of the side, one foot with an untied black Converse high-top shoe on and one foot left bare, while eating Quaker Oats Apple Cinnamon-flavored oatmeal from a green single-serve microwavable cup. I'm on my hefty inch-thick pink Dell laptop, with a red external hard drive hanging out of a USB port off to the right that appears to be falling off the edge of the mattress.

I was searching for the right song to play next, despite being very late to leave for a party the marching band was throwing off-campus, about a mile walk down the side of South Mountain.

Today, I don't know where that music library is or if that external hard drive still functions. iTunes is being deprecated, which breaks my nostalgic heart but makes me realize that I don't know the last time I actually used it.

My music collection transformed alongside a rapidly changing recording industry:

- 1995: a cassette tape of Robyn's hit single, "Show Me Love"
- 1996: a compact disc of Donna Lewis' *Now in a Minute* played on repeat on a Sony Boombox (apparently, you can still purchase a Boombox from Best Buy for $99)

- 2001: waiting an hour for the latest LFO song, "Every Other Time" to download from Napster in order to play it using Windows Media Player (with the visualizer, of course)
- 2007: using a cassette to 3.5 mm headphone converter to listen to my iPod full of illegally acquired Something Corporate songs on the way to high school
- 2009: my college roommate, Julia, photographs my iTunes plus external hard drive setup; my future employer, Starbucks Coffee Company, doles out codes to redeem free downloads from iTunes of soon-to-be hits like Phoenix's "1901"
- 2012: Spotify spreads like wildfire in the US and I almost entirely abandon Pandora's ship for the "starred" playlist feature, combining the powers of both services by finding new music on Pandora and saving it for anytime play on Spotify; I discover Matt and Kim's "Daylight" this way (three years late) and overplay it
- 2015: I'm addicted to Spotify but start my own vinyl collection of albums that I want to listen to all the way through, like X Ambassadors' *VHS*
- 2020: my one-bedroom apartment in a South Boston triple-decker has an unnecessary number of Sonos speakers for the low square footage, and I have experienced Andrew McMahon play "Dark Blue" at fourteen shows in five different US cities

I still find myself running late because I need to listen to *one* more song, but how I find and if I own that song has changed. These changes in how we consume and listen to music have shaped the industry into what it is today.

CHAPTER 3

PIRATES

"So, pirating destroyed the music industry, and now it's slowly recovering with streaming services," Tucker Jennings replied nonchalantly when I asked him what he meant by the "new" music industry.

Tucker is a drummer and songwriter from NYC, currently playing in the pop duo DREAMDIVE. Though succinct, he put it well. Providing the general public with the ability to easily pirate music over the internet for free effectively destroyed the recorded music industry.

In the years that followed Napster, the industry as we knew it imploded and slowly re-emerged as something very different. I believe we are hitting a point of potential implosion again today, and depending on how fans and artists collaborate in reaction to this change will shape the response from the industry.

If done right, artists and fans may be able to reshape an industry that makes it easier for creators to earn a living.

THE LILLYWHITE SESSIONS

I experienced the power that fans had been given by the "new" music industry of the early 2000s firsthand. I was only eleven, but I knew then what I know now—big changes are afoot.

In 2001, the Dave Matthews Band (DMB) released *Everyday* and loyal fans like my dad and I didn't love it. It has grown on me since, but it still sticks out like a sore thumb in their catalog because it is primarily Dave Matthews on guitar, whereas their other music is multi-instrumental and relies more heavily on other parts of the band. I think the only other album that is different from their collection when considered as a whole is *Stand Up*, released in 2005, but that album still features the rest of the band more prominently than *Everyday*.

Shortly after *Everyday* was released, my dad found a leaked copy of most of what eventually became *Busted Stuff* but was then known as *The Lillywhite Sessions* on Napster. I recall that there were rumors that the band's label pushed Dave Matthews into writing *Everyday* because it wanted a more commercialized, poppy DMB and that they found the songs on what would be later released as *Busted Stuff* to be too dark because he was emotionally distraught from the murder of his sister.

The rumor went that the label asked Dave Matthews Band to produce *Everyday* without Steven Lillywhite but instead with pop producer Glen Ballard as quickly as possible. They finished the album in ten days.[61] Fans were outraged and the internet revolted, leaking the unfinished songs from *The Lillywhite Sessions*.

Rolling Stone covered the leak in 2001 and explained away the rumors:

It's a myth that the big, bad record company came down and said, "Where's the hit"...That's absolutely incorrect. There are plenty of songs on that unreleased record that are going to be big commercial singles. No one—Steve Lillywhite, Bruce Flohr, Dave Matthews—no one knew that Glen Ballard and the band were gonna go on such a creative spurt that the songs that were originally recorded were going to be put aside.[62]

In an interview with *Billboard* from when *Busted Stuff* was released, Dave Matthews backs up this report from *Rolling Stone* that "after months of... 'tension and banging one's head against the wall,' the tracks were scrapped, and the band linked with producer Glen Ballard to record Everyday."[63]

I can't help but wonder if *Busted Stuff* might not be a part of the released Dave Matthews Band catalog today if it had not been for the fans who leaked it over the internet. This was

---

61 "Dave Matthews Band's 'Everyday' Turns a Page," *Billboard Magazine*, February 9, 2001.
62 Greg Heller, "The Long, Botched Summer: The Birth, Death and Rebirth of a DMB Album," *Rolling Stone*, July 11, 2001.
63 "Dave Matthews Band Revels In 'Busted Stuff,'" *Billboard Magazine*, June 7, 2002.

the first time I remember experiencing the power of fans to change the industry's cycle or way of doing things.

THE (FREE) EMINEM SHOW

Sitting at the breakfast bar in my sticky, hot apartment on an August evening, surrounded by boxes in preparation for my classic Boston September-first move,[64] I chatted over a rough VoIP connection with Chance and Tucker Jennings—manager and artist, brothers in arms, fighting their way to the top of the charts.

I scheduled a twenty-minute call with them but we ended up talking for over twice that time, catching up as former classmates from high school in Connecticut and sharing thoughts about which artists would play our imaginary perfect concert bills. Laughing a little, Tucker shared, "I can't think of a third, but if Coldplay and Hans Zimmer did a show together, I'd be all about it."

We got off track throughout our conversation, discussing Blink-182's tour with Lil' Wayne, a matchup we consider interesting but confusing, and how I found Call Security, Tucker's former band, via Spotify before knowing I had gone to school with its drummer.

---

[64] Madeline Bilis, "The Best Time to Sign a New Lease in Boston Is During Winter," *Boston Magazine*, January 29, 2018. As of 2018, "80 percent of leases turn over on September 1st" in Boston. It is a chaotic time to move because the entire city is blocked off with parking permits and filled with U-Haul trucks.

Chance and Tucker described two different industries throughout our conversation about success—old and new. When I asked them to elaborate on what they meant by the "new" industry, with ease they recounted experiencing the same pivot point in history that I recall as a kid of the '90s: the "old" industry is anything pre-1999 or pre-Napster, and the "new" industry is what has resulted from the shift in consumer behavior that Napster brought.

Chance and Tucker gave me an inside scoop about the clear order to releasing new music in the "old" industry and explained how each industry actor had his/her role. The cycle went something like:

1. Record new album (songwriters, audio engineers, producers, record label executives, manager)
2. Go on tour to promote the new album with a crazy press release schedule and PR in record stores (marketing, press management, talent bookers/venues, booking agencies, promoters)
3. Release new album (record manufacturers, distributors, warehouses, stores)
4. Continue touring or go on a second full tour (tour management, roadies)
5. Go back into the studio while album sales revenues support you for a few years (see step 1)

Pirating and peer-to-peer networks like Napster destroyed this cycle. The albums were already recorded, engineered, and being pressed into CDs at factories around the globe while they were being promoted on the album release tours. Consumers were eagerly anticipating "New Music

Tuesday"—when freshly shrink-wrapped jewel cases would hit shelves of music stores across the country.

Pirates aimed to release the music as soon as it hit shelves, if not before, hurting the effect of "New Music Tuesday." It meant everyone got the music faster and hackers got internet street credit.

In *How Music Got Free*, Stephen Witt demonstrates this cycle breaking down best with the example of Eminem's *The Eminem Show*.[65] The album was set to be released on June 4, 2002, but it was leaked by the team of hackers that Witt follows throughout his book.[66] The team of hackers, "Team Rns Presents," released *The Eminem Show* early on May 10, 2002, noting that, "Even though it would go on to become the year's bestselling album, the rapper was forced to reschedule his tour."[67]

It makes sense that Eminem would have to reschedule his tour, as Tucker explained in our interview that in the old model, "The tour was a way to promote an album release, an album release is where all the revenue is generated, and now it's essentially the opposite."

As mentioned in chapter one, recording industry data reflects this trend: record sales took a huge dive from 2003–2011,[68]

---

65 Witt, *How Music Got Free*, 140-141.
66 Witt, *How Music Got Free*, 141.
67 Witt, *How Music Got Free*, 141.
68 "US Recorded Music Revenues by Format," RIAA, last accessed January 27, 2020.

and income from live music tours increased over that period to recoup revenues.[69] Album releases and touring were so intrinsically linked until the mid-2000s that when one went through change, the other had to follow.

NEW INDUSTRY

Chance and Tucker explained that in the "new" industry, there is less of a need to rely on a complex contract with record labels or distributors because the infrastructure they provide is much less relevant. It is easier for creators to remain independent and self-funded. For example, Chance said, "because of modern technology, people can get a pretty good studio setup for pretty cheap, and so many people are now making their homes their studios." In a recent Forbes article, songwriter Danny Ross outlines the equipment one would need to record and produce music for as low as two thousand dollars in an apartment.[70]

Recording studios have become so obsolete that even famous ones, like Sound City Studios in Los Angeles that worked with acts like Tom Petty and Nirvana, have shuttered their doors.[71] From 2007 to 2016, employment in the sound recording industry fell by over 40 percent.[72]

---

69 Krueger, *Rockonomics*, 25-26.
70 Danny Ross, "How to Be a Hit Music Producer With a $2,000 Budget," *Forbes*, September 21, 2018.
71 Samuel Stebbins and Evan Comen, "America's 24 Dying Industries Include Sound Studios, Textiles, Newspapers," *USA Today*, updated January 4, 2018.
72 Ibid.

Further, the internet has made distributing recorded music easier than ever. In the past, artists needed access to physical distributors of recorded music with factories, warehouses, and a supply network. Today, online distributors and platforms such as Spotify or Apple Music replace those physical distribution channels. Creators can upload music to Spotify and other services in a matter of days[73] by creating a profile on the platform and submitting music via a distributor.[74]

Run River North, previously known as Monsters Calling Home, famously recorded a music video in their Honda because they didn't have a studio or other space (the video later landed them a spot on Jimmy Kimmel Live! and appearance in a Honda ad). In a video sponsored by Honda, they explain, "We don't have a studio, we're not really signed anywhere, so let's just use what we have. We just like literally fit a drum set into a Honda Fit."[75] Though "the total cost to produce a professional music video can range from $20,000 to $500,000,"[76] with today's technology and distribution channels like YouTube, anyone can make a decent quality video on a low budget.

Sometimes, the old industry cycle is completely reversed—"[c]oncerts are now viewed as a primary profit center, and

---

73 "How Long Does It Take for My Album to Be Available in Stores?" DistroKid, last accessed January 27, 2020.

74 "Provider Directory," Spotify for Artists, accessed January 27, 2020.

75 "Honda Surprising Monsters Calling Home," Honda Trinidad, September 25, 2012, video, 00:35.

76 "How Much Does It Cost to Make a Music Video," Indigo Productions, Video Production Blog, posted on August 23, 2013.

digital recordings are a means of promoting concerts."[77] Artists release parts of an album to streaming services to support a tour that is already planned rather than the other way around. Though tons of work goes into writing, recording, producing, and marketing an album, which I doubt will ever change much, creators have more control than ever given the ease of releasing music online today versus via physical media in the past.

For example, New York City-based indie-pop band MisterWives released a five-song EP *mini bloom* in late 2019 to support their "No Place Like Home" tour so that fans would have new music from the upcoming album before seeing them again live. Mandy Lee Duffy, lead singer and songwriter for MisterWives, explains in an interview about the EP, "We put it out; really, last-minute… It's more of a party when everybody's getting to sing together as one than knowing four or five songs that we're playing."[78]

As a fan who went to a show from the "No Place Like Home" tour in December 2019, I can attest to the brilliance behind this strategy. The crowd danced and sang as loudly to the new songs off of the *mini bloom* EP, like the Cranberries-esque "the end" and the emotion-filled breakup ballad[79]

---

77 Krueger, *Rockonomics*, 19.
78 Roman Gokhman, "Q&A: MisterWives 'Bloom' Again with New Music and More on the Way," *Riff Magazine*, November 21, 2019.
79 Mitch Mosk, "MisterWives' Unapologetic 'WhyWhyWhy' is a Dynamic Post-Breakup Reckoning," *Atwood Magazine*, August 1, 2019.

"whywhywhy," as they did to past hits such as MisterWives' very first, "Reflections."

Today, artists still release new music according to the new industry standard of "New Music Friday," but they can put out several EPs, singles, or albums without much pre-release hype or press. Most of that press comes from social media and appearing in playlists on streaming services.

Without revenues from traditional record sales to rely on, artists are touring more often, but tours are no longer necessarily tied to an album release. "Many artists used to treat touring as a loss leader, a way to… promot[e] record sales… [hoping] to sell enough records to score another lucrative record contract,"[80] but today that paradigm is no longer. Instead, the opposite occurs in which artists release music in hopes of driving more ticket sales, which are now their bread and butter.

CALL SECURITY
Not only do artists defy the old industry cycle by releasing music and touring when they want or need to, but some artists also strategically use this newly broken cycle to their advantage by releasing music for other reasons.

For example, some bands release new music on a specific cadence in an attempt to make it onto Spotify's algorithm-created playlists, learning what works best through trial and error. These algorithms break songs down into

---

80 Krueger, *Rockonomics*, 19.

pieces and analyze patterns in songs to generate playlists of similar styles. Now, combined with user data, these playlists help listeners find new songs and artists based on their past listening behaviors.

Though many playlists on Spotify are generated automatically for the individual based on his/her tastes, the team at Spotify does curate some playlists, to which artists can submit their songs: "You can submit an upcoming, unreleased song for our team to discover and consider for editorial playlists."[81]

Foregoing touring altogether until it makes more economic sense, DREAMDIVE's release strategy is focused on trying to make it onto these Spotify playlists to accumulate followers early and to generate revenue to cover studio costs. DREAMDIVE's manager, Chance Jennings, explained that Spotify's product is shrouded in mystery, since "no one really knows how the algorithm works," but that doesn't deter him from trying to crack the code.

Chance explained to me that once the band gets picked up by the algorithmic playlists, hundreds or even thousands of potential new fans can be reached per week. Then, if those fans like the song—and they *should* if Spotify's algorithm got it right—the platform will continue to push that song in similar playlists, until it ultimately will begin pushing any new songs from the band to those fans.

---

[81] "How Do I Get My Music on a Spotify Playlist? Submit Music for Playlist Consideration," Spotify for Artists, FAQ, last accessed January 27, 2020.

"Those are just invaluable tools as a small band," Chance explained, "because you can just get your music out there. If you're able to get on some of those algorithmic playlists, it can be a consistent and continual source of exposure that never really dries up."

The approach that Chance, Tucker, and the rest of the DREAMDIVE team take in methodically releasing music, managing the band's social media presence, and strategically planning shows is borne from the "new" music industry that they described to me on our call. Tucker's "golden rule" is to always make sure that anything the band does drives them toward success and isn't being done just because "it fits in with all these antiquated myths about how the music industry works and how bands 'make it.'"

Time will tell if this strategy works out for DREAMDIVE. Though operating in a rigid and outdated industry, there are many actors still making money off of creators opting for a more traditional route than DREAMDIVE.

In the next chapter, I'll break down who's who in the music industry and how they help the artist write, record, sell, and tour on their music.

CHAPTER 4

WELL-OILED MACHINE

When I first realized how difficult it is for creators to earn a living from their work, I vilified everyone in the industry who stands to make money off their music. I felt like the industry machine was taking a lot from my favorite artists but giving them very little back. I wanted to find a way they could live without any help from the industry.

I was not alone in having anti-industry or anti-record label feelings. Similar to the anti-big label feelings that fueled fans' fire and pushed them to leak Dave Matthews Band's *The Lillywhite Sessions* mentioned in chapter three, negative feelings toward those with power in the music industry initially contributed to the spread of illegal music downloading.[82]

An academic study conducted in 2005 aimed at understanding the tendency toward or away illegal music downloading found that "supporters of the file-sharing system hold

---

82 Chun-Yao Huang, "File Sharing as a Form of Music Consumption," *International Journal of Electronic Commerce* 9, no. 4 (2005): 49.

that big labels and 'the whole mass of media dictatorship' represent a 'system' that exploits consumers."[83] The study found that those who illegally share music via services akin to Napster of the late 1990s typically "justify their behavior with reference to the perceived egregiousness of record companies."[84]

Consumers felt that their actions were similar to that of the popular Robin Hood legend[85] in which Robin Hood steals from the rich to give to the poor, thereby exonerating him for his crime of stealing. Those who steal music feel that they are not hurting anyone as the harm is not readily apparent, which is a common issue with intellectual property theft, or if they knew they were harming someone in their stealing, these thieves felt justified because they were stealing from record label monopolies.[86]

As I will get into later in this chapter, it is not untrue that record labels have, in some cases, committed acts that were bad for artists and bad for consumers. However, stealing music from major artists can have a real impact on the success of emerging artists because of how record labels manage their money. For example, stealing music from the likes of Dave Matthews Band may seem harmless because the band has made so much money, but the reduction in revenue from their music trickles down to result in a lack of investment

---

83   Huang, "File Sharing as a Form of Music Consumption," 40.
84   Ibid.
85   Ibid.
86   Huang, "File Sharing as a Form of Music Consumption," 49.

on the part of the label in new artists.[87] In the late 1990s and early 2000s, this created even more of an issue than it does today because the labels had a monopoly on the means of production, i.e. artists could not do what Run River North did and record their albums in their cars because the sound quality would be atrocious.

I ultimately found that it was completely unrealistic to believe that any creator could "make it" without a little help from his or her friends in the industry. Though later in this book I'll provide examples of some changes I believe certain parts of the industry could make to better serve artists, there are several industry actors who help artists succeed.

So, who's who in the music industry?

WHO'S WHO

Herein is a high-level dictionary to help you navigate the rest of this book. It does not cover every single person who could be involved in getting your favorite hit single to your AirPods, but this should be enough to give you an idea of who's who in the music industry. Keep in mind that most emerging artists have a pretty bare-bones team, so they might not interact with all of these people when they are first getting started.

---

87 Krueger, *Rockonomics*, 20.

CREATORS

I use the term "creator" frequently. When I speak of creators in this book, I do not only mean the musical acts themselves, like X Ambassadors or Taylor Swift, but I also mean those who contribute to the music creation process, such as songwriters, collaborators, and producers. As I will elaborate further below, sometimes the same person or group of people accomplish(es) most or all of these various "creator" functions when making a song.

Some industry insiders I spoke with while researching for this book would stretch the "creator" definition even further to include those who reproduce others' work in performances, i.e., playing in an orchestra or a wedding band. Oftentimes, those musicians will have a personal take on a work of music, thereby creating something new. I wholeheartedly agree that it's an art to be able to perform in those capacities. I also believe those musicians deserve to be paid fairly for their hard work and it should be a career path that allows them to provide for themselves and their families.

However, for the sake of simplicity, this book mostly deals with those I have defined below, which make up the majority of popular music that the average listener consumes.

Performing Artists (or "artists")

This one is pretty self-explanatory: performing artists are the Taylor Swift, X Ambassadors, and Ed Sheeran-types who perform music for recording or live shows. When we think of rock stars, we typically picture the performing artists.

Songwriters

Songwriters develop the lyrics and musical composition for a song in "the process of putting musical ideas together to form a larger structure of coherent melody, harmony, and rhythm."[88]

Some performing artists are also the songwriters of their works. For example, Taylor Swift writes or co-writes all of her own music,[89] so she is both the performing artist and the songwriter of her music. I'll explain why this is particularly important for Taylor later in chapter seven.

In the case of MisterWives, most of the songs are written by front-woman and lead vocalist, Mandy Lee Duffy, though some other bandmates are credited with writing some of the songs and she has started to collaborate with other artists, like Sir Sly, on their newest material.[90]

Determining who the songwriter is matters when trying to figure out who gets paid and how much they are owed when divvying up royalties—I'll dig into this more in chapter six.

---

88 Yoni Leviatan, "Making Music: The 6 Stages of Music Production," Waves Audio, Blog, July 27, 2017.

89 Travis M. Andrews, "Can Taylor Swift Really Rerecord Her Entire Music Catalogue?" *The Washington Post*, August 22, 2019, Pop Culture.

90 Kelly McCafferty, "Real Songs, Real Talk, and Real People: A Conversation with MisterWives," *Atwood Magazine*, October 28, 2019.

Producers

Producers develop the song from the concept brought forth from the songwriter into a full song. They direct the performance and instruct the audio engineers during the recording process. Producers are like extremely talented project managers—coordinating all of the pieces and injecting advice or direction where needed to help produce the best final output.[91]

Performing artists may insist on producing their own music as well, in which case an artist could take on all three of these roles.

Other creators worth mentioning

There are several other people involved in the music creation process from back-up performers to audio engineers. Without these additional people, the end result wouldn't be as great as the songwriter, performing artist, and producer intends it to be, so they are integral to the process.

INDUSTRY

Managers

Managers, like Seth Kallen and Chance Jennings, are jacks of all trades. As Seth Kallen put it in our interview, "Your role can be completely different depending on where the artist's strengths are and what they're trying to do." He went on

---

[91] "What Is the Difference Between the Producer, Engineer, and Mixer?" Outerloop Group, February 19, 2019, video, 00:48.

to describe this role as the "captain of the ship" since "the manager is the closest person to the artist."

Essentially, managers are there to support the artist with whatever they need to be successful, from booking shows to babysitting.[92]

As the artist's career grows, the manager's job evolves from doing everything to building a team of people around him or her to support the artist in various capacities, from branding to social media marketing to booking gigs.

Managers are typically the first hire for artists[93] as they are getting started, but it is fairly common for artists to forego this step and manage themselves. For example, Patreon co-founder, Jack Conte, wrote in a Medium blog post in which he broke down the revenue and costs of a tour for his band Pomplamoose, "[b]ecause Pomplamoose doesn't have a manager, Nataly coordinated the logistics of the tour, herself. On top of that, we recorded and released a full-length album."[94]

Other team members working on behalf of the artist
Depending on how successful the performing artist becomes, he or she may need more teammates to help

---

92 Donald S. Passman, *All You Need to Know About the Music Business*, Ninth Edition (Simon and Schuster, 2015), 16, Kindle.
93 Ibid.
94 Jack Conte, "Pomplamoose 2014 Tour Profits," Medium, November 24, 2014.

manage the business. These could range from a lawyer to review contracts, an agent to help field syndication requests, a business manager to take care of financials, and a press or media manager to deal with press requests and public relations.

That is just a short list of key folks a typical artist would have as dedicated team members or at least part-time advisors, but there are likely even more people involved as the artist grows in success. Each of these teammates is typically paid a cut from the artist's share of revenues.

Record Labels

Deals with record labels provide artists with help in creating and selling their music, from advertising to recording studio time. Although variable based on the record label company and agreement, record labels provide support in various forms, from resources to money, to the artist, typically in exchange for the rights to the master recordings. Master recordings (or "masters") are "the original copies of an artist's work."[95]

Not all record label agreements grant the rights to the masters over to the label, as Taylor Swift recently signed a new contract with "Universal Music Group's Republic Records in a multiple-album agreement that allowed her to own her future masters."[96] Other artists have regained control of their

---

95 Joe Coscarelli, "Taylor Swift Says She Will Rerecord Her Old Music. Here's How." *The New York Times*, updated August 27, 2019.
96 Ibid.

master recordings in the past as well. For example, "Prince vowed to re-record his entire catalog while feuding with his label, Warner Bros., in the 1990s, but released only select tracks before reaching an agreement to gain ownership of his masters."[97]

Larry Miller, a professor of music entrepreneurship at New York University,[98] once compared agreements with the record labels with agreements to accept venture capital as a startup. In his comparison, he explains that the master recordings are akin to the equity a budding startup would give to investors in exchange for capital or resources.[99] He explains that record labels "make investments in unproven talent,"[100] just as venture capitalists take a chance on the founders of a new startup. In the end, if the artist or startup is successful, the revenue from the masters or cashing in on the equity gives the investor a return on his/her investment.

Artists do not necessarily disagree with Professor Miller's stance, but they hope to find ways to regain control of their master recordings later once they achieve success. Instead, they find it's nearly impossible to do so depending

---

97 Ibid.
98 "Larry Miller: Clinical Music Associate Professor and Director, Music Business Program," NYU Steinhardt, last accessed January 27, 2020.
99 Joe Coscarelli, "Taylor Swift Announces New Record Deal With Universal Music," *The New York Times*, November 19, 2018.
100 Coscarelli, "Taylor Swift Announces New Record Deal With Universal Music."

on their existing recording contracts.[101] Further, power in the recording industry is highly concentrated, which makes it even more difficult for creators to negotiate a fair contract.

I'll dig into why agreements with record labels over who owns master recordings of performed works matters in my case study of how Taylor Swift is challenging the status quo of today's music industry in chapter seven.

Apart from the disagreement over who should retain ownership of artists' masters, some of the animosity toward the record labels comes from the fact that there are now only three major record labels with most of the power—Sony Music Entertainment, Warner Music Group, and Universal Music Group. As of 2016, those three record labels controlled "62.4 percent of all music sold, downloaded, and streamed worldwide."[102]

Booking Agents (and agencies), Promoters, Venue Management, and Talent Bookers (buyers)

Booking agents/agencies are often confused with talent bookers/buyers, but they are on opposite sides of the table. Booking agents work on behalf of the artist to get them gigs. Artists typically have their managers help them book shows

---

101 Ben Sisario and Joe Coscarelli, "Taylor Swift's Feud With Scooter Braun Spotlights Musicians' Struggles to Own Their Work," *The New York Times*, July 1, 2019.
102 Paul Resnikoff, "Two-Thirds of All Music Sold Comes from Just 3 Companies," Digital Music News, August 3, 2015.

or book on their own behalf until they have enough traction to convince a booking agency to take them on as a client. The agency then typically takes a cut from the band's income from shows it books. Most times, bands will retain the right to book themselves in case a show comes their way rather than having to always go through the agency and lose a portion of the show's income even for a show that the agency did not book.

Talent bookers (or talent buyers), on the other hand, source talent to book shows on behalf of the venue. Depending on the size of the venue, talent booking may be done by other venue management staff or even the owner. Typically, booking agents, managers, and/or bands reach out to a venue's talent booker in an attempt to book a gig. There is unusually high turnover in talent booking because really good talent bookers are often moved up through the ranks to bigger and better venues.

Promoters have a tricky job in the middle of talent bookers and booking agents. A promoter takes a chance on a bill of bands and coordinates with the agents and the venues to get shows booked. Promoters are like general managers of the concert—they handle everything related to putting on a show from advertising to booking. The promoter typically takes on the financial risk in this scenario as well, and he or she is incentivized to sell as many tickets as possible. Live Nation, for example, is actually described as "the world's largest concert promoter"[103] despite also owning

---

103 Josh Mandell, "Where Does Live Nation Have Room To Grow?" *Forbes*, March 4, 2019.

some music venues and managing ticketing platforms like Ticketmaster.

In recent years, large management groups, like the Bowery in New York City, have acquired several venues, and the talent booking function is performed at this group level. Boston has a division of Bowery as well, which owns and operates nearly every small live music venue in the city.

When I was first researching how artists become successful, I was particularly interested in understanding why some of my favorite artists moved up the ranks of the Boston live music scene. As I am sure you have noticed in your own city, I could see that there was a clear order in which venues were played as the band grew in success: starting at small divey clubs like the Great Scott in the college neighborhood of Allston and ending at giant arenas like the TD Garden in downtown Boston. Sometimes bands were able to skip levels, rising to fame much quicker than their peers. Other times, I noticed bands getting stuck at the same level, playing five-hundred-person capacity venues like Brighton Music Hall over and over again but never making it to the next tier.

In our interview, artist manager Seth Kallen validated my hunch, explaining that, for example, in New York City, "Bowery Presents is not going to let you play at Terminal 5 unless you show them that you can sell out Webster Hall because, at the end of the day, it's all about demand." Venues are businesses that need to make money, so this makes sense. Venues need to know they can sell tickets and drinks to cover their costs, so they book shows that seem the most likely to turn a profit. I still could not help but wonder how artists got in the door in the first place and then how they worked their way up.

I found that despite all of the advances in technology and transformations in the industry, one aspect that remains as difficult and as manual as ever is booking live shows. This is particularly true for small, independent venues and new, emerging artists. The onus is on the artist to pursue talent bookers at venues to book them, and sometimes venues will request that the artist help sell tickets, pay-to-play, or find their own local opening act. Other times, venues will completely ignore artists who lack a history of playing that city or do not call it home.

THE GOOD GUYS
Most of the time, a creator's success is tied closely with the success of those who work for him/her in the industry, but not always. I'll dive into how parts of the industry need to change in chapter eight; not all of the people working in the industry are unfairly profiting off of creators.

Throughout this journey into the black box of the music industry, I was fortunate enough to interview a few industry insiders who are trying to help creators be successful and who care deeply about the fans:

- Becky Blumenthal, marketing manager for Live Nation in Philadelphia

- Seth Kallen, founder of This Fiction Management and manager to bands like X Ambassadors, Jukebox the Ghost, and Great Good Fine Ok
- Chris Walkowski, tour manager for Andrew McMahon

In chapter five, I will provide profiles, advice, and stories from my interviews with Becky, Seth, and Chris.

CHAPTER 5

BEHIND THE VELVET CURTAINS

The lack of transparency in the music industry often obscures more than just financial data and contract terms—it also hides amazing people who work tirelessly to further artists' careers. As I mentioned in chapter four, I was so outraged by how difficult it has become for artists to make a living that I channeled that anger toward the industry as a whole. As I dug deeper, I found smart, compassionate, and dedicated people working behind the velvet curtains to provide fans with amazing experiences and to build creators up.

Though I interviewed so many interesting fans, artists, entrepreneurs, and people in the industry, these three people each perform very different jobs in the industry, but each convinced me that there were industry actors truly looking out for creators.

BECKY

I felt like I could ask Becky Blumenthal anything. Becky is the marketing manager at Live Nation for the Philadelphia region, and though she has an intimidating résumé and impressive knowledge of all things music or music industry, she is friendly, outgoing, and supportive. We ended up talking on the phone for nearly an hour and a half. She is so kind, in fact, that at the end of our long talk she offered to help me in any way she could—with the book, with my career, with anything.

Becky started in the music industry at a very young age, playing in bands at summer camp in her teens. "I was never very good, and I didn't really yearn to be on stage," she said assuredly. "I always, always wanted to work on the side, to help get bands into venues." At that age, I had no idea what I wanted to do. I tossed around the idea of being an astrophysicist, a chemical engineer, or a Supreme Court justice (none of which panned out, obviously).

Yet when Becky was telling me about some of her background, it was very clear that she knew she always wanted to work in the music industry. She wanted to help artists succeed and provide unforgettable experiences for fans: "I've done all of it. I just knew that I always loved music. I didn't think twice about it."

Becky Blumenthal has done it all. While completing her undergraduate degree at Barnard College in New York City, she interned at Sony Music, one of the "big three" record labels I mentioned chapter four. She jumped around from department to department at Sony, working in publicity, business development, finance, or wherever she was needed. Upon graduation, she landed a job working at the startup WeMix.com, led by the rap artist Ludacris.

Two years later, Ludacris's company closed its doors, so Becky went back to school. She went on to complete a master's degree in history from Rutgers, and later an MBA from Temple University.[104] Throughout and after graduate school, she worked in marketing and market research but never stopped having a passion for music. She continued to see a ton of live music and would help bands make websites to market themselves as her side gig.

In 2014, her friends bought Ardmore Music Hall, a live music venue in Ardmore, Pennsylvania, which is perfectly situated on the "Main Line" right outside of Philadelphia and near several colleges. They approached her to join their team as the marketing director. "So, I quit my job," Becky told me in a matter-of-fact manner, as if there was no question in her mind about what to do next.

In the five years that Becky worked for the owners of the Ardmore, the group expanded to owning and operating four venues and ran a few successful music festivals. Simultaneously, she worked for an independent music label, GroundUP Music, started by the band Snarky Puppy,[105] up until joining Live Nation in May 2019.

---

104 "Becky Blumenthal," LinkedIn, last accessed January 27, 2020.
105 "About," GroundUp Music, last accessed January 27, 2020.

Becky has worked for a major label and an independent one. She helped bands get booked at venues and then booked shows for her own venues. She has built festivals from the ground up, worked in live music promotion, and has done marketing for every part of the music business. She worked in every time zone and said yes to every opportunity, ultimately booking shows in Australia, Bulgaria, and Bolivia.

When given the chance to join the marketing team at Live Nation, which is pretty rare at her level, she jumped at it: "I had been interested in stepping it up, doing bigger and bolder things with more money."

At Live Nation, the premier concert promoting and ticketing company in the world, she is able to step it up. I was taken aback when she shared the fact that "there is a Live Nation concert every twenty minutes." A few other statistics Becky shared with me make it clear that Live Nation offers her a chance to operate on a bigger scale. It:

- Operates in four continents,
- Holds over twenty-five thousand events per year, and
- Has privileges in at least three thousand venues.

Honestly, I had not thought of Live Nation in this way before I spoke with Becky. I always associated the company with the seemingly exorbitant ticketing fees that I pay when I buy my tickets online. Becky is no stranger to this criticism, but she meets it head-on with some good points about working for a larger company versus a small indie place.

Becky explained to me, "I'm still coming in as a fan so I care about their experience, but now I can make a positive impact via music on the lives of thousands of people a year because I'm working in bigger spaces." Just looking at the numbers, when she worked for Ardmore Music Hall and other venues, she impacted maybe five hundred people a night. At Live Nation, if her team does its job right, they could potentially share music, sports, and/or comedy with fifty thousand people per night. It is not often that someone gets the chance to multiply their ability to make an impact by a hundred times overnight.

Her desire to provide a great experience for fans does not stop at numbers—she is also a huge proponent for the ways that Live Nation gives back to fans, as she shared with me that the company aims to give out discounted or free tickets to active fans regularly.

Moreover, Becky is excited about the bands that Live Nation takes a chance on and supports in the industry. She loves being a part of something larger since "most bands don't dream of playing to a hundred people; they want to play to twenty-five thousand people, and I want to see a band I work with ultimately get the opportunity to play places like Red Rocks or The Gorge or Carnegie Hall."

Becky brings several years of expertise to the table, providing artists with advice such as:

- "Sell music with music" by advertising using digital clips of a band playing live so the fan knows what to expect.

- Be conscious of the timeliness of your band name—she gave me the example of the band Cosby Sweater, whose name is now associated with defamed Bill Cosby, which is not a good look.
- Build a cohesive brand for fans to follow—like the warpaint that Walk The Moon members wear on stage and die-hard fans sport to shows or the nine-piece funk band Turkuaz from Brooklyn in which each member of the band wears the same color every night and in every picture so even though their name is challenging, their rainbow image is easily recognizable for fans searching for them.

Becky's role at Live Nation is essential in helping artists grow. Touring is more important than ever in the streaming economy, and Becky's team helps promote artists so their shows sell out, thereby generating more revenue for the artists. In an age when artists have to wear several hats, a helping hand is welcomed.

For example, musician Miranda Mulholland from earlier in the book says, "I'd really prefer to just be writing music and performing music and doing my main job,"[106] but she can't be successful without having to wear several other hats and promote herself:

[I have to] update all of my gigs on all of my websites, my Facebook, my Instagram, keep people engaged, give them just enough but not too much, make my life look interesting but not

---

106 Miller, "Mind the (Value) Gap," 13:57.

give everything away...there's such an amount of not creating that I have to do day to day.[107]

Becky takes on the role of some of these hats by helping artists promote their gigs and making sure that fans have an amazing experience at shows. She works tirelessly "to get people off of their phones" so that the crowd does not have to watch the show through the phones blocking their view, an experience to which I am sure we can all relate.

Live music concerts are magical. They are important events at which people can connect in today's world absent the church communities of old, as Becky pointed out, "We're not nearly as religious of a population anymore, and so concerts are one of the places where people gather to communicate and to share something in common."

SETH

Seth Kallen runs This Fiction, a successful artist management company out of New York City. I was elated when Seth agreed to do an interview with me because he manages some of my very favorite artists such as X Ambassadors, Savoir Adore, and Great Good Fine Ok.

When I called Seth for our scheduled chat, I caught him in between meetings, calling from his car. As anyone can tell from his Instagram, Seth is seemingly always moving about—from LA to NY and in between—going wherever he needs

---

107 Miller, "Mind the (Value) Gap," 13:41.

to in order to support his artists. Seth loves that as an artist manager, "every day is completely different."

Seth got his start in artist management when he discovered Jukebox the Ghost at a George Washington University concert. When he saw Jukebox play, he knew they had talent and offered to manage them.[108] After attending New York University, Seth rose through the ranks at MCT Management before breaking off on his own and starting This Fiction.[109] He took Jukebox the Ghost with him to This Fiction and then started working with talented artists from the very beginning of their careers, the same way he did with Jukebox.

On our call, Seth told me about his experience helping bands like X Ambassadors go from playing small rooms with barely a crowd of twenty to selling out Red Rocks. I shared with him that I actually attended some of the shows he mentioned and as a fan, it was awesome to hear from the other side how much being at that show meant to the artist as a milestone in the band's career.

Despite spending his entire career successfully helping artists grow, Seth casually says everything in the industry is still trial and error, but he offered some advice to bands, fans, and managers:

- "Every step you take should be purposeful." Artists should always ask why they are doing something, whether it's

---

108 Ross, "How to Manage Pop Stars."
109 Ibid.

playing a show or releasing a single and what it does to further them in reaching their goals.
- "Go build something on your own." If you can't get a gig at Bottom of the Hill, for example, throw a bunch of free house parties in San Francisco until you have enough of a fan base there, and then ask them to show up for you. Fans—when a band asks you to show up, do it! It means more to them than you could ever know.
- "Try to book on a night of the week that you know no one else is trying to book a show." If you can't get into a place or you're struggling to book gigs, approach the venue with an offer that works for them by picking a night that you know they struggle to sell out, promising a crowd, foregoing a guarantee, and then delivering on that crowd of fans.
- "Every fan counts. There's so much music out there, and people are consuming music now more than ever. Don't only focus on the streams and social media; make real relationships with your fans."

To wrap up our conversation, I asked Seth for his favorite moment of being a manager. He audibly hesitated and pondered, ultimately struggling to answer because so many came to mind. Though qualifying that there are many moments he could share, he recounted that he was "filled with gratitude and really happy" when he collaborated on Cayuga Sound Music Festival with X Ambassadors in 2017. Cayuga Sound Music Festival takes place in X Ambassadors' hometown of Ithaca, New York. He said he did everything with the band to put the best show on, from hand-picking the food vendors to coordinating a series of panels for students at Cornell and Syracuse.

"X Ambassadors got to go back to their roots and they surprised their elementary school with a show in the cafeteria—it was a combination of everything I loved about working in music all in one weekend," he said. The festival is also special because profits are donated to charity. Since we had just finished talking about how to help bands be financially successful, Seth laughed a little when he told me that the work that he and the band put in versus the financial benefit made no sense. Yet, thankfully it went really well in the end so that they were able to turn a profit and donate.

The lack of financial benefit does not deter artist managers like Seth Kallen. He clearly cares deeply about all of the artists on This Fiction's roster and their communities and looks for ways to give back to those communities whenever possible.

For example, Jukebox the Ghost puts on a show each year around Halloween called "HalloQueen" in which they exclusively play Queen covers. Seth told me of one year when he went to HalloQueen at a sold-out thousand-capacity venue with the audience in costumes singing along with Jukebox the Ghost to Queen covers, and he thought to himself, *Is this really my job? This is so fun.*

CHRIS

Speaking of fun jobs, Chris Walkowski has one of my dream jobs as Andrew McMahon's tour manager. I began following his public Instagram account years ago when I realized that he was tagged in most of Andrew McMahon's tour photos so I could see more behind the scenes-esque footage by following him. I am a huge Andrew McMahon fan, if that's not already clear, and I have followed his music through his various bands since high school, from Something Corporate to Jack's Mannequin, to Andrew McMahon in the Wilderness.

Andrew McMahon has a powerful story because he was diagnosed with leukemia in 2005 at twenty-two years old and survived. Since his survival, Andrew started the Dear Jack Foundation, which helps young adult cancer patients and survivors and holds an annual concert to raise money for the foundation. I went to the annual Dear Jack Foundation benefit concert in Denver in 2017 and in Boston in 2018. It was so moving to contribute to such a great cause and hear the stories of cancer survivors that Andrew brought on stage. At the show in Boston, Andrew played "Konstantine," a nine-and-a-half-minute song that he never plays (I've been to fourteen shows, and I have only seen it played live once), and I was brought to tears.

I was dying to meet someone behind the scenes of Andrew's elaborate productions—someone helping Andrew put together these amazing shows night after night. Though an entire team is involved, I found that Chris Walkowski is a key part in making sure all of the pieces fit together.

Chris started out his career by going to school in Michigan for Music Industry Management and then interning for Crush Music in New York City. He worked closely with Andrew McMahon's manager (his version of Seth Kallen), Rob Hitt. Rob gave Chris the chance to go on tour with Andrew and act as his merchandise manager, and after a few years of hard work, Chris was promoted to tour manager.

Tour management sounds hard, but Chris makes it fun. Though he is responsible for coordinating who the crew will be for the tour, booking a tour bus and a truck for transporting the gear and the sets, booking hotels and fun days off with a travel agent, production plans, and advancing the show with each venue (that's all?), he makes sure that the band and the crew have a little fun along the way.

He said that the team starts every day in a new city on the hunt for the best coffee place,[110] and though I was sad to hear that they haven't had a chance to experience all that Boston has to offer by way of good coffee, he shared that his favorite place so far is Snowing in Space in Charlottesville, Virginia, which specializes in nitro cold brew.

Chris plans fun activities for the crew for off days, like the time that he and the team got off of a twelve-hour flight to Japan, grabbed food, and then immediately went to a place called "Mari-Kart" where they were able to dress up as fictional characters and drive go-karts through the city:

It was late at night, raining, and we are actually on the streets of Tokyo. Cabs and cars are passing us. We ran some stoplights due to the size of our party, and, at one part, outran the cops through little alleyways that only a go-kart could fit in. It was hilarious and amazing.

---

110 "An Interview with Tour Manager Chris Walkowski," StageRight, July 10, 2019.

Touring is not always as fun as driving go-karts through the alleys of Tokyo, however. I asked Chris about one of the most surprising things that happened to the team when they arrived at a venue, and he told me of a time on the "Upside Down Flowers Tour" that their tour bus broke down. The team was stranded in the middle of nowhere, three hours from their destination, and he was researching alternative ways to get the entire crew to the venue. Thankfully, someone from a local shop showed up to fix the bus and they made it to the venue in time for the show, but he was worried about setting up the elaborate sets that Andrew used.

I went to see the "Upside Down Flowers Tour" at the House of Blues in Boston, and as I was hanging on the edge of my seat to read how the show went on in Chris's email to me, I recalled that the set for this particular show was extraordinary. The piano was tucked underneath a second story, where other bandmates played, and the entire structure resembled lifeguards at a pool, since "upside-down flowers" are beach umbrellas. At one point in the show, the set transformed, revealing the piano and Andrew McMahon.

It is not easy to transport a piano, let alone such a decorative two-story set. Chris said that though the bus broke down, the truck with the sets and gear was able to get to the venue ahead of the team and work with the local crew to set up for the show, so doors were only delayed about thirty minutes.

Chris's stories are important in the lesson that touring is difficult and takes a lot of manpower, and some luck, to put on the amazing shows fans experience night after night.

Chris's final advice to fans is simple:

I wouldn't have a job if it wasn't for the fans. Just go to shows and support the bands you love! Also, watch the opening acts. Usually, they are awesome and you'll be happy you got there early to watch them and maybe find a new band you love.

In the next chapter, I'll explain how fans' money flows through the industry to pay Chris's salary and why it is so important for fans to go to shows.

PART TWO

CHAPTER 6

MONEY

Tucker Jennings, the drummer and songwriter from Brooklyn-based DREAMDIVE told me that he still works at a grocery store one day a week to make ends meet despite "pretty much living in the studio, just trying to get this next batch of music done."

Even with Tucker's past band, Call Security, the bandmates all had second jobs at Whole Foods or in restaurants in order to make their rent payments since "sustaining a full band on streaming revenues is challenging."

Call Security was not unsuccessful by many standards—the band was about to sign with a label when it ultimately dissolved and has a hit, "Small Talk," with nearly two million streams on Spotify. Yet, the band still could not afford to live off of streaming and touring revenues alone.

At the time of my conversation with Tucker and Chance Jennings, Tucker's second band DREAMDIVE had over 23,000 monthly listeners and a single on Spotify, "Can't Trust," with

290,000 streams.[111] Their branding and social media presence show a band in the studio and focusing on writing, but behind the scenes, Tucker works at a grocery store. You'd never know it, and that's on purpose, but Tucker is still shooting for success, which he defines as "when music pays all of [his] bills and it feels like something [he] can sustain [himself] with for years to come."

So how do creators make money in today's industry? Where does your hard-earned money end up when you buy a concert ticket or pay for a streaming service?

It involves some pretty shady and complex transactions. I've heard stories of being handed a wad of cash at the end of the night with no explanation as to how much it is or why or being asked to pay back fees after a show instead of making any money at all.

In either case, with the exception of advances, the only consistency I've found is that creators are the last ones to get paid, if they get paid at all. Further, as Alan Krueger points out in his book about the economics of the music industry, *Rockonomics*, "[m]ost of the money collected from recorded music does not go to the musicians who created the music."[112]

David Byrne of the Talking Heads wrote an op-ed in *The New York Times* regarding transparency in which he, a famous

---

111 Spotify Group, "Spotify: DREAMDIVE," DREAMDIVE Artist Profile, Spotify, Version 1.1.26.501.gbe11e53b (2020).

112 Krueger, *Rockonomics*, 36.

musician and someone I would have considered on the "inside" of the industry before I wrote this book, argued that:

Before musicians and their advocates can move to enact a fairer system of pay, we need to know exactly what's going on. We need information from both labels and streaming services on how they share the wealth generated by music.[113]

Byrne points to the lack of information flowing from record labels and music streaming services as well as "nondisclosure agreements"[114] created in order to keep the silence. Later, in an interview with Larry Miller on *Musonomics*, Byrne went further to explain that another reason artists remain in the dark about how they are being paid is because the record labels have not invested in technology.[115] He notes that the way artists currently receive royalty statements is outdated, and he is spot-on—artists receive "hard paper cop[ies]"[116] of hundred-page long summary reports.

Therefore, the following explanations are examples and are mostly meant to give you a sense of where your money is going as a fan but are not 100 percent accurate for every case. Given the lack of transparency in the music industry, even insiders struggle to explain how a ticket is split or how much per stream each artist or songwriter ends up making. Even more

---

113 David Byrne, "Open the Music Industry's Black Box," *The New York Times*, July 31, 2015, Opinion.

114 Ibid.

115 Larry Miller, "The Transparency Moment," September 2, 2015, in *Musonomics*, SoundCloud, podcast, MP3 audio, 2:16.

116 Miller, "The Transparency Moment," 4:04.

difficult than the lack of transparency is the great complexity and variability with how the money flows as well. Everything is on a case-by-case basis and "comprehensive, unassailable financial data for the music industry do not exist."[117]

ROYALTIES

In the Rethink Music project, researchers at the Future of Music Coalition and Berklee School of Music teamed up to build outflow maps[118] of how money makes it back to the artists. There are six three-part flow maps that I will do my best to give a high-level summary of here, but I encourage you to check out the maps for yourself at futureofmusic.org.[119]

Further, royalties from copyrights are currently in a state of flux with the new Music Modernization Act that was signed into law in Fall 2018, which I will dive into more later in chapter eight.

As of this writing, there are a few basic ways that creators (artists, songwriters, producers) can make money from copyrights and licenses. Let's start with streaming, since according to The Recording Industry Association of America (RIAA), streaming sources accounted for roughly $6.4 billion of recorded music sales in 2018 or approximately 65 percent.[120]

---

117 Krueger, *Rockonomics*, 29.
118 "Fair Music," Berklee, July 14, 2015.
119 Kristin Thomson, "Music and How the Money Flows," Future of Music Coalition, updated March 10, 2015.
120 "US Recorded Music Revenues by Format," RIAA, last accessed January 27, 2020.

Though streaming services are sometimes criticized for the amount that they pay artists, it should be noted that not all streaming services are created equally. Some services pay significantly less to artists than others, though the opaqueness of the payments makes it difficult to guarantee the accuracy of that claim. YouTube (Google) specifically has a bad reputation when it comes to paying artists fairly, whereas "Spotify, the largest streaming service, pays out approximately 60 percent of its revenue in music royalties."[121] Other experts, like Professor Larry Miller of NYU, claim that number is even higher, stating that "Spotify pays out 70 to 80 percent of its revenue to rights holders."[122]

Graham Henderson, CEO of Music Canada, put it as "the money that flows from one of the richest corporations in the world, Google, flows to performers and labels and everybody else at rates far, far below the market rate."[123] While it is challenging to say for sure what the difference is, Henderson estimates that Google pays only "five percent of the rate [paid by] Spotify and Apple."[124]

$0.00065[125] per play is a number that gets mentioned a lot when it comes to streaming. Some articles reported $0.00331

---

121 Krueger, *Rockonomics*, 32.
122 Larry Miller, "The Headwinds Facing Music Startups," June 7, 2016, in *Musonomics*, SoundCloud, podcast, MP3 audio, 13:37.
123 Miller, "Mind the (Value) Gap," 9:12.
124 Miller, "Mind the (Value) Gap," 9:50.
125 "Van Dyke Parks on How Songwriters Are Getting Screwed in the Digital Age," Daily Beast, updated July 12, 2017.

per play after averaging the various tiers.[126] Spotify is known to have two tiers, paying artists different amounts per play if the song is played from a customer's paid subscription versus from an ad-based, free-subscription plan.[127] Economist Alan Kreuger estimates that "a song typically earns royalties of around $2,000 to $3,000 per million plays."[128]

Whatever the rate may be, the money generated from one play of one song is typically broken down in the same parts, and how it reaches the creators depends on their specific agreements with labels, publishers, and others.

For example, right now I'm streaming "My Thoughts on You" by The Band CAMINO on my paid subscription of Spotify. First, depending on how many streams Spotify has in a given period of time and how many streams The Band CAMINO gets, The Band CAMINO and all parties that have an interest in "My Thoughts on You" will get paid the share of total streams related to the song. That's kind of a confusing concept, so I will break it down with a basic math example similar to what that Spotify uses in a video[129] to explain the concept to artists:

- Spotify has one million total streams in a given month

---

126 "2018 Streaming Price Bible! Per Stream Rates Drop as Streaming Volume Grows. YouTube's Value Gap is Very Real," The Trichordist, January 29, 2018.
127 "How Spotify Pays Artists," Spotify for Artists, November 15, 2018, video.
128 Krueger, *Rockonomics*, 32.
129 "How Spotify Pays Artists," Spotify for Artists.

- "My Thoughts on You" by The Band CAMINO has one hundred thousand streams in that same month
- For the sake of example, let's say this is their only song on Spotify (it's not and I highly encourage you to check them out, but after you read the rest of my book)
- The Band CAMINO then gets 10 percent of "the revenue pool"[130] because their portion of the total streams that Spotify had in the month is 10 percent

This gets even muddier when you consider that "the revenue pool"[131] according to a Spotify for Artists video, "How Spotify Pays Artists,"[132] could vary depending on if the consumer is listening to the stream on the premium (paid) service versus the free (ads-based) service.

To clarify, let's say in that same example, that the one million total streams happened over Spotify's free service. If the free service's ads-generated "revenue pool"[133] was one hundred thousand dollars, given the 10 percent share for The Band CAMINO, they would make ten thousand dollars from those streams. Simultaneously, The Band CAMINO still qualifies for payment out of the premium, subscription fees-based "revenue pool"[134] if a subscription user streamed their music over that tier of service, so they could be eligible for payment out of both tiers (though some artists and/or portions of catalogs are restricted to the paid service tier only).

---

130 Ibid.
131 Ibid.
132 Ibid.
133 Ibid.
134 Ibid.

Given the Van Dyke Parks example from my introduction, in which he co-wrote a song with Ringo Starr and estimated he'd make forty dollars from one hundred thousand plays on Spotify, I doubt The Band CAMINO, though fairly successful and on the rise, is making twenty thousand dollars a month from streaming.

Why? The money does not typically go straight to the artist from Spotify, depending on the agreement the artist has with its label and that the songwriter has with its publisher (the artist and the songwriter, though both considered creators in this book, may be different people).

Taking the fictitious ten thousand dollars from the previous example, let's assume that The Band CAMINO has a typical contract with a label as an up-and-coming (read: unproven[135]) act in which the recording studio owns the master recordings. For this example, let's also assume that The Band CAMINO collectively wrote "My Thoughts on You."

Per the Future of Music Coalition's flow charts, that ten thousand dollars would likely be broken down as follows:[136]

- A portion goes to the performance rights organization (PRO) that the band is a member of, as a stream is technically a "performance" of the work. The PRO then distributes it to the songwriter (in this example, that goes

---

135 Coscarelli, "Taylor Swift Announces New Record Deal with Universal Music."
136 Thomson, "Music and How the Money Flows."

back to the band) and the publisher, based on previous agreements that the PRO executes.
- 10.5 percent of this, minus fees to the PRO, gets sent to publishers for mechanical royalties, which is then sent to the songwriter based on the agreement between the songwriter and the publisher (again, in this example, some of the money goes back to the band).
- The rest goes to the band's label, which can ultimately pay the band 10–50 percent of its cut, depending on the terms of the contract between the band and the label.

The math is very messy because there are various branches off of which the money could ultimately make it back to the band, but it all depends on the contracts the band signed. Further, it is important to note that typically in those types of deals, the record label gives advances to the bands against which future royalties are earned, so the band may not see income after the advance for quite some time as they pay it back. Usually, the advance is "against a 10 to 12 percent share of future royalties, net of costs,"[137] and because "only one or two of every ten records that a record label releases actually covers its costs,"[138] it is unlikely that a band that does not find success will ever see income from their recordings past the advance amount.

In any case, the terms of contracts and ownership of rights are vital to getting paid, but even if the artist has the most favorable terms, the streaming services negotiate with the major labels and other entities individually (and without

---

137 Krueger, *Rockonomics*, 36.
138 Krueger, *Rockonomics*, 36.

artist input) to determine how they are paid.[139] Sometimes, the labels require that the streaming services pay large advances on royalties, for example, "[a] recently leaked 2011 contract between Sony and Spotify showed that the service had agreed to pay the label more than $40 million in advances over three years."[140]

Further, copyright laws play a unique role in how copyright payments are made. Though much of this will change with the adoption of the MMA, it is key to understanding why so many factions, typically on opposite sides of the table, came together to rally for change with the MMA. Until the MMA, royalty rates were set and managed by the laws. The 1909 Copyright Act "set the songwriter's fee for a mechanical royalty at 2 cents."[141]

Van Dyke Parks explains in his op-ed about "How Songwriters Are Getting Screwed in the Digital Age" that the two-cent royalty "was-relative to now-quite generous."[142] However, that two-cent rate did not change until the 1978 Copyright Act, which increased it to 9.1 cents to account for inflation.[143] As I mentioned in chapter two, the laws are often slow to be made and fall behind, typically hurting the creators the most as the record labels lobby Congress extensively.

---

139 Byrne, "Open the Music Industry's Black Box."
140 Ibid.
141 "Van Dyke Parks on How Songwriters Are Getting Screwed in the Digital Age," Daily Beast.
142 Ibid.
143 Ibid.

Though the sales of singles via digital download have been declining steadily since a peak in 2012—in 2018, the revenue from sales of digitally downloaded singles came in at $490.4 million, or 30.65 percent of peak at $1.6 billion[144]—Van Dyke Parks' op-ed does a great job of illustrating how money flows from the sale of a downloaded single:

A typical (non-physical) download costs 99 cents at iTunes. Of that, Apple (the distributor) takes 50 cents. Forty cents goes to the record label. Nine cents goes to the publisher. Record companies pay the artist's royalty out of its 40 cents, and the publishers pay the composer the slender 9.1 cents stipulated by the 1978 Copyright act.

Clearly, performing artists and songwriters are not making much income from the money fans spend on recorded music via digital downloads or streaming service subscriptions anymore, so how are they making a living?

LIVE SHOWS AND MERCHANDISE

Once I started to realize that royalties from music recordings were no longer creators' main source of income, I turned to look into touring revenues. I found that live music typically sustains artists, sometimes to their detriment.

In a week-long string of tweets about mental health, the state of the industry, and his next moves, Michael Angelakos of Passion Pit tweeted, "it's the 5th-anniversary of Gossamer,

---

144 "US Recorded Music Revenues by Format," RIAA.

an album that is about and the product of a manic episode. I nearly lost everything, including my life."[145]

Aiming to focus on his nonprofit, The Wishart Group, and his health, Michael explained that he planned "to be an artist with or without the industry."[146] Though many fans took to social media to reply with well wishes and support of Passion Pit, others misunderstood, prompting Michael Angelakos to issue a statement clarifying his plans. He elaborated, emphasizing the realness in his statement about nearly losing his life:

I cannot continue to operate in this space, this industry, due to the way that it functions and treats people that work for it or create within it. It does nothing to promote the health required in order to produce the work it sells. The risks associated with being a commercialized artist and embarking on a typical album release, like endless promotion and touring, have nearly killed me. People often throw these words around casually as well, but when I say that these requirements have nearly killed me, have killed many people, and continue to kill people; I am not stating a fact. I am speaking from a very real and personal place. I live this, and I watch other artists struggle with the friction between their health and their art.[147]

---

145 Michael Angelakos, "it's the 5th-anniversary of Gossamer, an album that is about and the product of a manic episode. I nearly lost everything, including my life," Twitter, July 23, 2017, 10:28 p.m.

146 Evan Minsker and Matthew Strauss, "Passion Pit's Michael Angelakos Not Done With Music, but Says the Industry 'Nearly Killed' Him," *Pitchfork Magazine*, July 24, 2017.

147 Ibid.

Michael truly wasn't throwing his words around. The stress of the industry has nearly killed him, but as an artist, he still needs to play by its rules in order to survive. It should not have come as such a surprise, then, that just a matter of months later in early 2018, Passion Pit was planning to tour again. Yet, many were surprised, because it seemed Michael Angelakos would never return to being a commercialized artist after his July 2017 statement.

Unfortunately, Michael could not afford to stay away from touring. He needed the live music revenues to help cover "the myriad costs of living with [his bipolar] disorder that nearly ruined [him]."[148]

Only two weeks before I saw him play at The Ogden Theatre in Denver, Colorado, Michael explained that touring is "virtually the only way the majority of artists make their money, [him] in particular."[149]

Passion Pit has continued to tour, with no signs of stopping, up until the writing of this book. I saw a show as recently as the summer of 2019 when I was fortunate enough to experience the *Manners* ten-year anniversary tour twice. As a fan who started sharing Passion Pit hit "Sleepyhead," it was an all-time moment for me.

---

148 Ilana Kaplan, "Passion Pit's Michael Angelakos on Speaking Out on Mental Health: 'People Just Want Me to Shut Up and Make Music,'" *The Independent*, January 11, 2018.

149 Ibid.

However great the performance, it was bittersweet to simultaneously know how hard it is for Passion Pit to be on the road and the potential mental, physical, and emotional toll it may be taking on Michael to be up on stage night after night.

This is the reality of the current music industry and why it needs to change. In order to afford to live, artists must tour. I am in no way advocating for the end of live music, but it must be more reasonable for artists to earn enough to live off of their music without risking their health.

This is not only the case for smaller artists like Passion Pit. I grew up in a household where Billy Joel was revered. Though the first concert I remember was Dave Matthews Band when I was thirteen, my actual first concert was before I was born—my parents went to see Billy Joel in 1990 while my mother was very much pregnant with me. Even for an artist as popular and successful as Billy Joel, who released music many years before the internet set it free, "more than 90 percent of his income was derived from live concerts [in 2017]."[150] That year, Billy Joel made a staggering "$27.4 million from live performances" compared to "only $1.3 million from record sales and streaming, and $0.6 million from publishing royalties."[151] Most performing artists are not in the millions, since "the top 1 percent of performers"[152] earn "60 percent"[153] of all "concert revenue."[154]

---

150 Krueger, *Rockonomics*, 36.
151 Ibid.
152 Krueger, *Rockonomics*, 14.
153 Ibid.
154 Ibid.

I was recently discussing this conundrum with a coworker of mine at a company social outing. He shared with me that he plays in two bands on the side of his full-time job at our company (which I could not imagine juggling); one band is more successful than the other. He explained to me that the more lucrative shows his successful band plays earn each of the bandmates about twenty dollars take-home pay at the end of the night, which is usually just enough to cover his gas and other expenses for the two-hour gig. When that is the case for so many emerging artists, not only is it challenging to make a living off of playing music but it is also difficult to generate enough profit to continue recording, releasing, and promoting music.

Though every show is different depending on the contract, in order to make it easy to understand where your ticket money is going, I will provide a typical breakdown of ticket incomes below.

Let's say you bought a $100 ticket to see your favorite new band. At that ticket price, we can assume your favorite band is playing a pretty big venue and is fairly successful, so for this example, we can assume they sell out a 3,000-person show at New York City's Terminal 5.

If everyone paid $100, then we can assume that the show brought in $100 x 3000, or $300,000.

A few problems arise with this example right off the bat:

1. Playing a big venue doesn't necessarily mean your favorite band is successful, i.e., they can support themselves on music alone.

2. Typically, fans pay different ticket prices for different access or depending on from where they purchase the ticket.
3. Not all 3,000 people will buy a ticket—some will get them for free from the promoter, artist, label, venue, or other industry participants.
4. Terminal 5 is actually going to give the band a better deal than other venues because of its ownership "because it's owned by a local promoter, Bowery Presents, much of the infrastructure—stagehands, lighting, sound, security, things a band would have to pay for elsewhere—is in place…[so] 'bands can make a higher percentage of the earnings in that one room than in any other room in NYC.'"[155]

So, of that $300,000 generated,

- 10 percent, or $30,000, goes toward "a booking fee and a processing fee"[156]
- 5 percent, or $15,000, goes toward taxes (in the US; this is different abroad)[157]
- Roughly 1 percent, or $3,000, goes to "licensing agreements"[158]

---

155 Jacob Ganz, "The Concert Ticket Food Chain: Where Your Money Goes," *NPR News*, April 6, 2011, The Record.
156 Eamonn Forde, "Where Concert Ticket Money Goes: Who's Getting Rich off of Live Music's Golden Age?" *The Guardian*, January 30, 2017, Music.
157 Ibid.
158 Team Jukely, "Where Does Your Money Go When You Buy a Concert Ticket?" Jukely, April 30, 2018.

- "Anywhere from 25–40 percent of the ticket"[159] sales revenues, or $75,000–$120,000, goes toward paying the venue staff
- Depending on if the show had a promoter involved, "the promoter is going to take anywhere from 5–15 percent to advertise the event,"[160] or $15,000–$45,000
- Whatever is left of the pie ends up with the band, but that portion typically has to cover "their production crew, sound, lights, transportation…and manager"[161]

A pie chart illustration of this example:

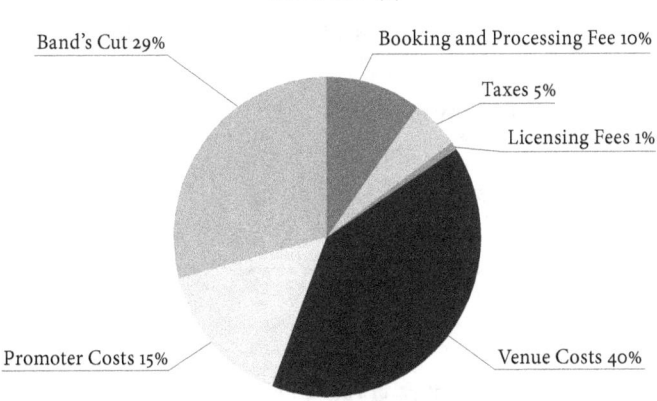

Amount ($)

Band's Cut 29%
Booking and Processing Fee 10%
Taxes 5%
Licensing Fees 1%
Venue Costs 40%
Promoter Costs 15%

Founder of Patreon and member of the band Pomplamoose, Jack Conte, published tour income and costs in 2014[162] to

---

159 Ibid.
160 Ibid.
161 Ibid.
162 Jack Conte, "Pomplamoose 2014 Tour Profits," Medium, November 24, 2014.

illustrate the ways in which the band's cut of the sales can be broken down. Jack reported that Pomplamoose's cut of the revenue was $135,983 after playing shows in venues like the Fillmore in San Francisco, which has a capacity of 1,315 fans.[163]

He broke down in his Medium article that:

- 72 percent of the tour's income came from ticket sales[164]
- 22 percent came from merch sales[165]
- 6 percent came from a sponsorship from Lenovo[166]

However, the artist is the last to be paid, and at the end of their tour, they ended up $11,819 in the red.[167] How?

The band had to pay for:

- Production expenses
- Hotels
- Food
- Travel
- Insurance
- Merchandise cost of goods sold
- Advertising
- Booking agency commissions
- Salaries and per diems

---

163 Ibid.
164 Ibid.
165 Ibid.
166 Ibid.
167 Ibid.

In the end, $48,094, or about 35 percent of the revenue, went to salaries and $20 per diem for each bandmate (six touring bandmates) and the crew.[168] None of that money went to Pomplamoose. Further, Pomplamoose is an anomaly—they don't have a manager or a tour manager who would normally get paid from the band's cut of the ticket sales.[169]

A pie chart illustration of the money Pomplamoose spent on the tour out of their cut of ticket sales:

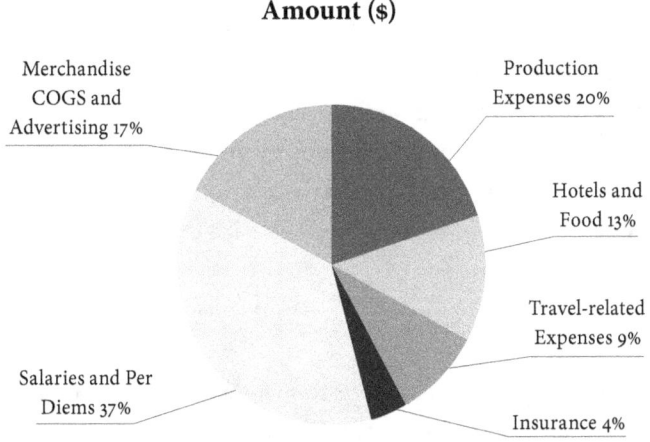

Amount ($)

- Merchandise COGS and Advertising 17%
- Production Expenses 20%
- Hotels and Food 13%
- Travel-related Expenses 9%
- Insurance 4%
- Salaries and Per Diems 37%

As Jack's example shows, even when a band sells out shows at thousand-person capacity music halls, they may not turn a profit.

---

168 Ibid.
169 Ibid.

SYNCHRONIZATION

A final source of income worth explaining because though small, it is increasingly important, is synchronization revenue from licensing works for use on television shows or in commercials. Synchronization revenue "accounts for only 1 percent of all music revenue,"[170] but with the expensive cost of touring and lack of income from recording revenues, artists are turning to synchronization more often for help. Seth Kallen supports the benefits of synchronization revenues, citing the success it brought X Ambassadors given that the advance check from a sync deal paid for their tour van.[171]

Another benefit of synchronization is the way that it takes advantage of a different channel to advertise on behalf of the artist. When I interviewed superfan Kenny Cohen, I asked her how she finds music, and one of the first ways she mentioned was through looking up the soundtracks of television shows.

WHY NOW?

The most important first milestone for a determined creator is the ability to make music a full-time job and their real career. The opacity of the music industry has made it difficult for creators to know if they are being paid all that they are owed and how the money flows through the industry back to them. When the money does make it back to the artist, it has already gone through a gauntlet of costs and most of

---

170 Krueger, *Rockonomics*, 33.
171 Ross, "How to Manage Pop Stars."

the time, it still is not done being divvied up among the interested parties.

These problems have plagued creators for years.

So, what is so special about this moment in time that I think we can make big changes for the better?

CHAPTER 7

WHY NOW?

People have been asking for change in the music industry for years, but never before now has the moment been as ripe for real systemic change. There are five key precipitating factors, referenced throughout the book, that make now the right time for change:

1. Artists are shirking the conventions of the music industry without sacrificing success—Chance the Rapper foregoing a record deal and instead partnering with SoundCloud to release his music for free
2. New ways to play live music and connect with fans in person are bringing artists and fans closer together—Sofar sounds
3. The use of social media to share details about closed-door deals and raise awareness of the issues in the industry have started to increase transparency—Taylor Swift's negotiations with Universal Music Group and conflict with Scooter Braun
4. Industry actors from all sides, creators, tech companies, and lawmakers came together to agree to changes to US

copyright laws—the passage of the Music Modernization Act (MMA)

CHANCE THE RAPPER

Recently, some artists have foregone the major record label and remain unsigned, like Chance the Rapper. Chance the Rapper has shirked traditional industry practices to become "the most successful free agent" in rap history, adding amendments to some how-to-make-it-in-music rules and rewriting others entirely.[172] Chance rose to stardom by releasing most of his music for free on SoundCloud[173] rather than selling it through traditional means, "buil[ding] up a singular reputation for remaining unsigned to any record label and for dropping his songs online for free."[174] Further, in 2017, Chance the Rapper "became the first artist to win a Grammy without selling physical copies of his music."[175]

Chance the Rapper's success without a music label is iconic. He leveraged the internet to share his music with fans for free, thereby lowering the barrier to entry for fans to reach his music. He recognized the shift away from touring to promote an album to releasing music to promote a tour early on and capitalized on the momentum built from sharing his music for free to generate income from live music.

---

172 Jayson Greene, "Chance the Rapper 'No Problem' [ft. 2 Chainz and Lil Wayne]," *Pitchfork Magazine*, May 13, 2016.

173 Dee Lockett, "Did Chance the Rapper Just Save SoundCloud?" *Vulture*, July 14, 2017.

174 Amy X. Wang, "Why Chance the Rapper—Who Just Made Grammy History—Gives His Music Away for Free," *Quartz*, February 13, 2017.

175 Ibid.

Chance's success demonstrates that artists can "make it" without the big record labels, primarily on the backs of fans attending shows and by leveraging modern technology.

SOFAR SOUNDS

Sofar Sounds is an online platform that coordinates secret live music shows all over the world. The shows are typically "held in a unique venue, like someone's living room or an antique shop,"[176] and primarily focus on connecting artists to fans.

I interviewed Matt Brooks, regional director of eastern North American operations for Sofar Sounds, about how he believes Sofar is changing the music industry for the better. I met Matt through a friend and colleague at a monthly game night. It was actually my turn to host, and he was so friendly that I felt comfortable asking him for an interview after hardly knowing him.

Matt says that Sofar is unique because the event is set up to encourage artists and fans to connect. The "intimate"[177] setting outside of the traditional music venue forces artists to get creative and play with different instruments or sing without microphones. The lack of stage, heavy instrumentation, or amplification equipment forces fans to pay attention and listen carefully to the music. Further, the sets are kept short and the bands mingle among the audience during the other artists' sets and after the show.

---

176 "Homepage," Sofar Sounds, last accessed January 27, 2020.
177 Ibid.

Sofar is important in changing the industry in more ways than just providing a setting for fans to meet other fans and artists. Sofar is revolutionizing live music in two key ways:

1. Sofar Sounds shows do not violate radius clauses[178] because they are secret. This allows bands to play in cities that would typically violate such a clause, which means that bands can both generate more revenue from touring and they can drum up support for their future shows at the Sofar set.
2. Sofar sometimes provides artists with the opportunity to capture video of a live performance in a unique space. Videos of live performances are key components of electronic press kits used for landing future live music gigs. These videos can also be uploaded onto social media as a marketing tool for the band to attract new fans. Further, Sofar will sometimes promote the artists on its website, which is essentially free advertising.

In my conversation with Matt, he summed it all up with, "The mantra that we say at Sofar a lot is that we want to help artists quit their day job."

TAYLOR SWIFT

It should be no secret that Taylor Swift is a force to be reckoned with in the music industry. She is an unstoppable star

---

[178] Radius clauses are typically included in any major touring or venue contract to prevent cannibalization of ticket sales by restricting where artists may perform concerts within a time frame and physical distance or radius from the venue in question.

with a highly dedicated fanbase of millions of listeners. What may not be as obvious, though, is the way that Taylor has been able to make waves in the music industry for the better, all whilst still generating fame and fortune for herself.

Recognizing that streaming "services pay less in royalties than she would [receive] from full album sales,"[179] Taylor postponed providing such services with access to her album *Reputation*. She recognized that her die-hard fans would buy her record instead of waiting for it to become available via streaming platforms and that those who waited likely would not have bought a copy of the album in the first place.[180] Relying on the connections she has made with her fanbase, primarily using social media platforms such as Tumblr and Twitter, Taylor Swift has been able to continue to profit off of recorded music in an age when almost no artist can.

Her power goes beyond her business aptitude, though. Taylor has figured out how to wield her social media power in other ways to her advantage. For example, after her master recordings were sold to Ithaca Holdings, headed up by Scooter Braun, in the acquisition of her former record label, Big Machine Label Group, she shared her discontent with her loyal fanbase on Tumblr, writing that the deal "stripped [her] of [her] life's work."[181] She told fans that she was considering re-recording all of her past work since she will own

---

179 Krueger, *Rockonomics*, 34.
180 Ibid.
181 Joe Coscarelli, "Taylor Swift Says She Will Rerecord Her Old Music. Here's How."

her master recordings per her new contract with Universal Music Group.

Taylor can re-record her entire catalog, with few exceptions, because she is credited as the songwriter on all of her own music. Since Taylor's current catalog generates a great deal of revenue, if she could shift her entire fanbase over from listening to the recordings owned by Braun to the re-recordings owned wholly by her, she would severely damage Braun's business.[182] Given her success in selling music to a modern music consumer who has almost entirely stopped buying or owning music, her ability to draw her fanbase away from the old recordings and toward the new may not be as challenging as it might seem. Within a matter of years, she could, as one fan on Tumblr said, "make [the masters Scooter bought] worthless."[183]

Taylor Swift recently used Twitter to further expose what is typically kept behind closed doors by posting a plea for help. She revealed in a post about being bullied by Scott Borchetta, the head of Big Machine Label Group, and Scooter Braun, that Scott and Scooter were preventing her from performing at the American Music Awards ceremony awarding her with Artist of the Decade. She claims they "said that [she's] not allowed to perform [her] old songs on television because they claim that would be re-recording [her] music before [she's] allowed to next year."[184]

---

182 Ibid.

183 Ibid.

184 Taylor Swift, *Don't know what else to do*, November 14, 2019, 6:35 p.m., photo, Twitter.

Capitalizing on the attention, she goes further in her post to reveal that Netflix is working on a documentary about her but Scott and Scooter are preventing them from using her "older music or performance footage."[185] Taylor asks for her fans' help in letting Scooter and Scott "know how [they] feel about this,"[186] leaving fans with this sentiment:

I feel very strongly that sharing what is happening to me could change the awareness level for other artists and potentially help them avoid a similar fate. The message being sent to me is very clear. Basically, be a good little girl and shut up. Or you'll be punished.

This is WRONG. Neither of these men had a hand in the writing of those songs. They did nothing to create the relationship I have with my fans.[187]

Taylor's willingness to reveal what is normally kept in the black box of the industry ultimately led to her being able to perform at the ceremony. Her performance highlighted the conflict, featuring a costume change in which she came on stage wearing a white prison-like jumpsuit with the names of her past albums written across it and *Fearless* written across her back.[188] She tore the jumpsuit off before beginning to play one of her old hits, the master recordings of which Ithaca Holdings now undoubtedly owns.

---

185 Ibid.
186 Ibid.
187 Ibid.
188 "Taylor Swift—Live at the 2019 American Music Awards," Taylor Swift, November 26, 2019, video, 00:40.

MUSIC MODERNIZATION ACT

As I have eluded to up until this point, passing the Music Modernization Act (MMA) in October 2018 took a monumental effort from all corners of the music industry. Not only did lawmakers in a very divided Washington, DC have to agree, but typically conflicting factions in the industry had to compromise. This is one of the rare times in history that all of these competing interests aligned to make changes to how copyrights are managed in the digital age.

The bill has a few major components that should transform the music industry. Larry Miller, director of the Music Business Program at NYU highlighted these key parts well in an episode of his podcast:

1. "The MMA improves compensation to songwriters [by] streamlining how their music is licensed. It creates a blanket license for digital music service providers to offer permanent downloads and on-demand streams."[189]
2. The MMA "creates a Mechanical Licensing Collective to administer that blanket license" by "creat[ing] and maintain[ing] a public database of all the song's owners and percentage ownership of songs co-written by several writers."[190]
3. The MMA "makes sure legacy artists who recorded music before 1972 [will] be paid royalties whenever their music is played on digital radio."[191]

---

189 Miller, "How Music Got Modernized," 2:21.
190 Miller, "How Music Got Modernized," 2:37.
191 Miller, "How Music Got Modernized," 3:09.

4. The MMA "provides a way for producers and engineers to receive royalties for their contributions to the music they helped create."[192]

With the creation of blanket mechanical licenses and the Mechanical Licensing Collective (MLC), the MMA eliminates the ability for streaming services to file forms in the US Copyright Office claiming difficulty finding the rights owners who are owed royalties. The changes from the MMA are still being enacted, but the requirement of blanket licenses and the MLC will effectively obliterate the black box of unpaid royalties that I mention in the introduction. Artists will finally get paid what they are due.

More symbolically, the cooperation among creators, record labels, lawmakers, and streaming services demonstrates the dire state of the music industry leading up to the MMA. This dire state pushed enemies together to make concessions in order for a better industry for all.

Still, despite steps in the right direction with Chance the Rapper's success, Taylor Swift's transparency, Sofar Sounds' growth, and the passing of the MMA, the industry is not done changing.

---

192 Miller, "How Music Got Modernized," 3:20.

CHAPTER 8

CHANGE

Now is the time for fans, artists, entrepreneurs, and the industry to come together to make big changes for the future of music. We have seen unprecedented levels of cooperation among these groups in recent years. Transparency is more common than ever with the rise of sharing on social media and the new MMA requirements. We need to strike while the iron is hot.

INDUSTRY AND ENTREPRENEURS

As I mentioned in chapter four, a few parts of the industry must change. Instead of investing in technology, the recording industry primarily focused on using expensive lawsuits against streaming services and pirates in an (unsuccessful) attempt to stop the recorded music revenue ship from sinking. Though the Music Modernization Act is a step in the right direction, I believe that some of the old industry actors have quite a ways to go before being truly "modernized."

There are two easy ways that entrepreneurs can collaborate with industry folks to become truly part of the modern age:

1. Royalty statements should be sent to consumers in a digital format and managed with data analysis software.
2. Talent booking should be streamlined and managed by a consolidated software solution.

First, as I mentioned in chapter six, artists are currently sent their royalty statements in paper copy form, meaning they have to manually analyze hundreds of pages of statements in order to make sure they have been paid properly and in order to understand their income from royalties.[193] As small business owners, creators need better and less time-consuming ways to be able to reconcile and analyze their revenues.

Second, as I mentioned in chapter four, talent bookers are using manual means of coordinating shows and taking huge risks when booking new, unproven talent.

Today, talent bookers sift through thousands of emails, calls, and Facebook to find the right talent. This forces the venue to impose strict rules about booking requests or to categorically deny gigs to bands via email autoresponders.

For example, the Bottom of the Hill in San Francisco, California, is so inundated with requests from artists that it has a long list of specific rules about contacting it for bookings on its site, like:

---

[193] Miller, "The Transparency Moment," 4:04.

- Do not send a note to our social media accounts; we use those for promotion only.[194]
- There is no phone number to call when making your introduction, but we do respond to your emails—if you do not receive a response, send a follow-up in a week or two. Remember to be patient with us because we get a large volume of inquiries.[195]
- Tell us what your fan base is like: are they under twenty-one for the most part and can't stay out past 10:00 p.m. on a school night? Or are they in their thirties and drink like fishes on any night of the week?[196]

Another venue, The Odditorium in Asheville, North Carolina, has an autoresponder for every email sent to its booking inbox that explains that you may not get a reply at all:

Hey friends! Thanks for contacting The Odditorium. I try to take the time to read every email that comes through, but if for some reason I don't get back to you within 5 days, assume that we are booked for the requested day or time. I'll be in touch within 5 days if I feel like we are a good fit for each other. <3 - Matt[197]

Though the requests from Bottom of the Hill and the autoresponse from The Odditorium seem harsh, these are typical for venues of their size (one hundred to four hundred-person capacity). The Bottom of the Hill site actually provides some

---

194 "Booking," Bottom of the Hill, last accessed January 27, 2020.
195 Ibid.
196 Ibid.
197 Matt Evans, email message to author, March 13, 2019.

pretty sage advice for bands hoping to play at their venue someday. However, putting together a professional electronic press kit and providing venues with all of the right information to show credibility is no simple task on top of everything else the bandmates are worried about, and it might not even get them the chance to play.

In my search for a technology solution for this problem, I found a database of venues online called Indie on the Move (IOTM), founded by two brothers who toured in the band ZELAZOWA. IOTM started as "a rolodex of music venues, booking agent contacts, venue reviews, and tour-related resources"[198] and "[grew] into one of the strongest musician communities on the web…based primarily on the idea that musicians working together…are typically more successful than those that go it alone."[199] IOTM offers "do it together"[200] resources such as a thirty-minute phone call with a booking expert for $175.

I took the bait and signed up for a call. I posed as an industry amateur looking to invest in a small venue in Denver, Colorado. I used the building across the street from my apartment as my muse when I took the call from the "Indie on the Move Pro." It was an old, abandoned brick building on Blake Street in the Ballpark area of Denver, behind Mile High Spirits and around the corner from Mile High Stadium. Despite its broken and boarded-up windows, padlocked entrances, and graffitied facade, it had character. It appeared to be an old

---

198 "About," Indie On The Move, last accessed January 27, 2020.
199 Ibid.
200 Ibid.

music shop of some kind and *Colorado Music* was painted across the side of the building in large, white block lettering. Who knows, I thought, maybe after speaking to this "Pro" (and hitting the lottery) I would be able to turn it into a venue!

The "Pro" was extremely knowledgeable and helpful, but he was adamant that the Google suite of tools like Gmail and Google Calendar were going to be vital to my operation because they were free and I would need them to organize all of my shows. Given that I had to use a paid tier of Calendly to organize interviews for this book, I could not fathom that the music venues of the world are planning shows entirely on the free versions of Google's apps, but apparently, they are—upon aggregating talent bookers' emails for a survey that I sent out in February 2019, most of them ended in @gmail.com—the "Pro" was right. I was bewildered.

I have spent most of my career in product management, building tools to help and empathizing with the small-to-medium-sized business owner. I intimately know the fear that small business owners feel about making ends meet, the high failure rate and personal credit destruction that failure can cause, and keeping track of every moving part all at once. I immediately felt empathy for the small venue a few blocks in the other direction from the abandoned brick building on Blake Street. There are so many expensive investments and challenges to running a venue, and apparently, a lack of tools to use to help the operation succeed. It started to make sense that venues in the area repeatedly booked local favorites on nights that were otherwise empty, and I wasn't surprised when I later heard that the owners of that venue down the way, Summit Music Hall, sold it, along with a few other venues in the area, to Live Nation.

Venues have tight margins and each show is do or die, so it makes sense that they fear taking a chance on a band that may not even bring in enough to cover the costs of running the show. However, the fear of this risk prevents them from taking chances on talent from out of town or which does not have the backing of a booking agent. Though artists can prove that they have a fanbase in various cities by tapping into streaming data and social media follower counts, this data is not perfectly correlated with the willingness to purchase a ticket to a concert. It is therefore considered but not wholly accepted as proof a band can sell enough tickets to cover the venue's costs.

Artists have worked hard to find ways around this risk aversion by taking on the risk themselves. They take the initiative, as per recommendations like that of artist manager Seth Kallen mentioned in chapter five, and negotiate less than favorable terms with venues to get in the door in order to build credit for a show later in their careers. Technology should be leveraged to increase data transparency and sharing across a network of venues to make booking talent less risky, thereby shifting the burden from the artists to a more equal place. Artists will always have to make the case to be booked, but venues can feel more confident in the risk it takes on new artists because they will be able to verify the artist's success at a similar venue in a similar market.

This data is available to large networks of venues owned by giants like Live Nation or the Bowery Presents but not to independently owned or smaller venues that are more likely to be the perfect places for new, emerging artists to play. In order to preserve the independence and existence of the local clubs that we love, we need to empower them with tools to make informed business decisions.

FANS AND ARTISTS

In chapter two, I told two powerful stories about connecting with the artist or with an audience through music:

- Simone Ellis connected with Demi Lovato over an emotional ballad from the very last row of the TD Garden arena.
- Becky Blumenthal connected with the diverse audience around her in a foreign country through lyric-less jazz music.

Though Simone claims that music does not play a vital role in her life, her stories say otherwise. Despite their differences in music taste, industry involvement, how they find new music, and more, Simone and Becky are *both* superfans.

Simone and Becky recognize the importance of connecting on a human level through music and the cultural value of that connection.

I spoke with many superfans in writing this book, and I found that fans are always at the center of change in the industry because fans are always in the center of the industry, period. As Chris Walkowski said in his interview with me, he would not have a job without *fans* seeing concerts. When

Taylor Swift took to social media to ask for help in convincing the industry bullies to let her perform at the American Music Awards, she asked her *fans* for help. Sofar Sounds is built on the premise that people are such big *fans* of music in general that it can sell out secret shows without revealing the artists on the bill ahead of time.

Fans are at the center of it all, and the cooperation of fans and artists will change the industry. I propose that fans and artists bond together and do the following:

1. Creators—emulate Taylor Swift. Do not be afraid to lean on your fan bases for support via social media or live performances when you want to stand up to unfair treatment or practices in the music industry.
2. Fans—be more patient and more present at live shows.
3. Fans—support live music at all stages.

Creators—share with your fans and don't be afraid to reach out for support.
Artists should be more transparent with fans about information that was previously kept in the black box of the industry in order to expose the areas that the industry needs to change the most. This transparency will harness the power of fans by swaying the industry to change when it needs to, as it did when Taylor Swift was able to perform her old music catalog at the American Music Awards show.

Fans—be more patient and present at live shows.
Concerts are not for everyone, but if you do attend a show, put your phone down and focus on being present in the

moment. The experience of seeing music played live is special and all-encompassing, and a lot of work goes into setting them up. Not only will the connection with the artist and the audience around you create a once-in-a-lifetime experience for you by bringing the music to life, but it will mean a lot more to the artist on the stage in front of you who is killing herself night after night in order to deliver a fantastic performance.

Chris Walkowski, Becky Blumenthal, and Michael Angelakos's stories illustrate how tirelessly performing artists and their teams work in order to bring fans an unforgettable experience, by spending months designing sets, building the perfect lineups, and traveling far from home for long stretches of time.

Furthermore, the artists *notice* when you are paying attention.

When I asked Katie Marshall of Paperwhite what her favorite moment was from playing music professionally, she didn't hesitate to share a story about the time she played at The Black Cat in Washington, DC. She told me that there was a moment when they were playing in which she noticed that people knew who they were, were singing along with their music, and had been at the show specifically to see them. It was the first show where she felt this strong feeling from the audience. "They had actually come for us," she said.

I researched the show she described and found that it was in May 2016, just a few months before I met her at Brighton Music Hall. I found a fan's account of the experience on her blog, and it mirrored how Katie described it. Paperwhite had broken the fourth wall, so to speak, and opened up about how much it meant to them to have the fans there to see them. The fan wrote,

Paperwhite's reaction to us (the audience) is just as awestruck as ours to them. Katie let us into her secrets, and we somehow did the same for her. Just by collectively releasing our inhibitions to enjoy a shared experience, we lowered the barriers between audience and artist. We had as much to give Paperwhite as they had to give us.[201]

This fan's blog post goes on to talk about how they met Katie after the show and talked about how "she didn't need to be so surprised that people deeply connected to her work."[202] She says "none of us are likely to forget [the concert]" and she was right, Katie hadn't forgotten the experience all these years later.

These moments of connection between artist and fan, though often vulnerable for the artist, are important to them too—Katie explained to me that these moments with fans keep her going through the ups and downs. She said that even my cold email asking her for an interview was one of the high points for her recently.

---

201 hello, witchsong, "Send Me Your Magic: Paperwhite Live in DC," Medium, June 2, 2016.

202 Ibid.

**Fans—support live music shows
for acts both big and small.**

Fans should go see the openers of their favorite artists and should attend concerts both big and small: showcases of local bands held by radio stations or at house parties, shows at the local club with capacity limits under five hundred, and shows at medium-sized theatres that help artists quit their day jobs.

Tucker Jennings of DREAMDIVE says that the fans who are present and participating in the show do more than propel the artist forward with positive reinforcement during tough times—they also stir up the crowd and make the live concert experience memorable for everyone attending, which increases the likelihood that they'll go to a show in the future.

Tucker believes that core fans create "this sense of excitement," turning the show into "a fun big event that could hopefully snowball from there" because people feel like they are a part of something bigger than themselves.

Tucker shared a story with me of a show Call Security played at Webster Hall in New York. The show was critical to their success because a label was attending in order to assess them. Chance and Tucker worked really hard to get their friends to come out and though they had a great turnout from a core group of fans, they got lucky in other ways too.

A large event was happening at the venue right after their show. Since their set time had been pushed back a little, a huge crowd of people from the prior event joined the show's audience, and "because fans were going nuts in the front, it turned into this massive, exciting show. [They] made a lot of fans that night because of the energy from the crowd."

I experienced this firsthand at a small show at Sonia in Cambridge, Massachusetts. A new artist, Eighty Ninety, opened for Savoir Adore. The room was practically empty, especially early in the night for their opening set. My friends and I arrived early, bought matching black pullover sweatshirts from Savoir Adore's lead singer Paul Hammer in the back of the venue, and lined up in front of the stage for Eighty Ninety's opening set.

Since it was our first time seeing Eighty Ninety, we had no idea what to expect. We listened to a few of the songs they released on Spotify to decide whether we would rush out of work to get to Cambridge early in order to catch their set. We liked what we heard enough to scarf down rosemary fries and PB&J's at Clover across the street. Yet, as people trickled in on the cold late-November Friday night, the room never really got packed and Eighty Ninety was playing to only a handful of interested people.

We were three of those interested people, but we tried to make ourselves count. Harper and Abner broke the fourth wall and told us that this was their first real tour and one of their first times playing live since they started recording music about two years before in 2016. As fans of small bands, knowing how hard they were working to make it, we couldn't let them down. We danced front row to every song and sang along when we knew the lyrics. We were the fans Tucker spoke of who were "going nuts in the front."

Once they finished their set, they began breaking down the set themselves, making way for Savoir Adore to set up. We went up to the edge of the stage to let them know that their set was great. After Savoir Adore's set, we met Eighty Ninety's Harper and Abner, and their parents. We left such an impression the band posted a photo on Instagram of the moment we chatted with them at the edge of the stage.

Live music is an incredibly important part of my life, but it only became so important since 2015, when I opened my mind up to the possibility of seeing live shows at smaller venues and even going alone.

Now, it is such a big part of my life that when I recently organized a big trip abroad, I chose dates based on the fall concert schedule in order to be able to see Flor and The Band CAMINO when they hit Boston. When people ask me how I can afford my live music habit, I always say that I'd rather spend ten dollars on a show at Great Scott, an old dive-y music hall in Allston, Massachusetts, than to see a movie or buy a fancy cocktail. When you do the math, going to a concert could be cheaper than seeing the latest *Star Wars* in the movie theatre.[203]

Some argue that they do not want to leave their homes to see live music shows. I completely understand social anxiety, being tired after work and not wanting to stay up late for a show, and, especially in the deep winter in Boston, the

---

203 I recently paid $15 to see *Star Wars* at the Arc Light Theatre in Boston. About a month later, I went to a concert at Brighton Music Hall for the same amount of money.

allure of staying in to binge-watch Netflix. However, when weighing your options consider a few things:

- Artists are traveling far distances in cramped vans and driving overnight, away from their homes for long stretches of time, to see you.
- When considering how tired you are from a long day of work, think of the two or more jobs that artists have in order to make a living while pursuing their passions. By attending a live music show, you are directly contributing to getting an artist closer to quitting his or her day job(s) in order to be able to make music his or her full-time career.
- Live music is good for our sense of community and social lives, which helps us stay connected with one another on a human level. I feel we could all use a bit more of this given how much time we spend behind screens nowadays.

I have felt that having met and known emerging artists has given me an additional appreciation for all of the hard work that goes into putting on a show for fans.

I interviewed Matthew Diamond, another superfan, who played in a band in high school that was successful enough to get a glimpse of the rough touring life of bands trying to make it. Though we didn't meet until about ten years later, I actually saw one of his band's shows at The Space in Hamden, Connecticut, when I was in high school because we had overlapping groups of friends (Connecticut is just that small).

Matt thinks his time in a band gives him a similar perspective when seeing shows:

We were really fortunate to play shows in various places in the Northeast. It's cool to get a small window into that world and now when I go see a local show, I have an understanding and an empathy with what those bands are going through. As far as you know, they're doing their own sound checks, hauling their own equipment, driving their own vehicles to the show. A lot of people who consume music don't see that side of the artists that they follow.

It is important that fans go to smaller live shows because they will see firsthand how difficult it is to make ends meet when an artist is just starting out. Though my book aims to build the same understanding and empathy that Matt is describing, seeing it live drives the point home that fans are directly linked to creators' success.

I asked other fans if they felt the same way and heard a resounding affirmation, time and time again. Jenn Lipes, a global HR project manager for Arcadis, says despite meeting tons of bands, from Walk the Moon to Young the Giant to MisterWives, one of the memories she'll never forget was the time that she met Sam Harris from X Ambassadors:

It was in Pawtucket, Rhode Island. There were literally 30 people at this show. In the end, Connor suggested that we wait for the band to come out. We waited a pretty long time, so we were not expecting it when they did finally come out. We didn't have anything for them to sign, but I had one of those Nike squirt water bottles so they signed my water bottle, and Connor only had Ocean Spray coupons, so they signed one of those. Later Connor tweeted at them with a picture of the coupon, "was going to get some juice but then realized I can't *possibly use this coupon. I like X Ambassadors so much, it's not worth saving the $2," and the band retweeted it.*

Now Jenn is an X Ambassadors fan for life, having seen them in multiple venues across the US and in Europe.

Another fan, Sunish Oturkar, who volunteers for Sofar Sounds from time to time, ended up helping out some pretty famous acts like State Radio after offering his professional photography services free of charge while he was in college. Sunish frequently went to see some smaller bands play various venues around Boston and noticed the lack of photography or merchandise help at the shows, likely due to the small size of the band. I have noticed this as well as some bands have manned their own merchandise booths at shows.

Sunish offered to help out with whatever these smaller bands needed, from manning the merch table to taking photos to even promoting their shows. He eventually went on to travel with one of the bands to help out on the road and was even mentioned in the acknowledgments of an album of another. He became close with the bandmates of one of the bands and told me an interesting story about a time when he was invited to a seven-course meal at the house of its bassist:

We would show up at seven p.m. and have seven courses that would take us through to three a.m. —it was just 20 people sitting in a living room with the chef and sous chefs. The bassist himself would cook these custom-made courses for you, and in between every course was some sort of cocktail that was tailored to the course itself. It was just random shit like that, that I got to do because I was involved in this music community.

Of course, I asked Sunish if the bassist made more money playing music or cooking. He speculated that given the state of the industry, though he was a talented musician, he probably made more money with his cooking.

CONCLUSION

"There's been a handful of times where I'm like, THAT was amazing. I mean, Florence & the Machine—Florence, she's one example. Her voice is even better live."
—JENNIFER LIPES, GLOBAL HR PROJECT MANAGER, ARCADIS, FAN

"You feel a little bit closer to the music when you listen to it later through Spotify or whatever because you've seen it live and you have that context. You're able to bring back the feelings that you had when you saw it live to when you listen to it recorded."
—CONNOR LEES, DIRECTOR OF RETAIL, BLANK LABEL CUSTOM CLOTHING COMPANY, FAN

"I feel that way about Young the Giant—Samir is such an amazing singer that I think he's even better live. I'll listen to the album and I'm like, gosh, the song is so much better live."
—KENNY COHEN, CUSTOMER CARE MANAGER, DELUXE CORPORATION, FAN

> "I feel like for any genre, if you really want to experience it, you have to go see it live—you can't listen to like heavy metal or dubstep on Apple headphones and think you know the genre. You just got to see it from within the whole community and all the energy behind it to truly understand it."
>
> —DEREK CLARK, COO, LABELRADAR, FAN

I'll go to great lengths to see a concert or to meet a band that I admire. I've taken a bus from Boston to New York City on a whim to catch a private SiriusXM-sponsored Chvrches concert in Brooklyn for their release of *Every Open Eye*. I then listened to the SiriusXM recording of that very show on the three-hour drive back to Boston for Boston Calling Music Festival with my friend Eric.

I've finished up my workday connected to a hot spot in the passenger seat of a rental car on I-90 heading west in order to see MisterWives at Terminal 5 in New York City and to attend their Medium Rare after party. I felt so lucky to hang behind the velvet ropes (literally) with the bandmates and congratulate them on another awesome performance.

Why? Because I am a **SUPERFAN**.

I am a superfan for the reasons the other music fans listed at the start of the conclusion. It sounds better live. It's a whole different experience. It's an experience that creates the type of close-knit community that Sunish mentions in his story about the seven-course meal in chapter eight, or the closest thing we have to being religious in today's society as per Becky in chapter five.

Obviously, attending multiple concerts per week, rearranging a trip to Europe around tour dates, or offering to go on tour with bands to shoot their professional photos for free are all a bit more than the average music fan or consumer is willing or able to do. However, being a superfan is not about the specific efforts that people put into helping creators quit their day jobs—it's about the intention to help creators live comfortably off of their work.

Being a superfan is not specifically about buying tons of merchandise, meeting the bands or getting autographs, but rather it is about making connections with others through music.

The stories and advice I have compiled in this book are meant to give you the power to be a superfan too. If every fan works towards becoming a superfan, the industry will see great changes very soon toward becoming a more equitable, artist-friendly, transparent, and technology-enabled community.

CHANGED FOREVER

I remember the first time I met a performing artist like it was yesterday. The whole night is seared into my memory as one of those moments that my life changed forever. It was July 17, 2015.

Once the lights came up, despite donning a light-washed denim mini skirt and a loose black tank —an outfit not conducive to any climbing activity of any sort—I jumped up onto the stage, scraping up my weak left knee in the process, and quickly crawled to the back right corner toward where

Louie's drum kit had been set up. On this tightly packed platform at the divey music venue Great Scott in Allston, Massachusetts, HOLYCHILD had just finished up their show and now I was on all fours tearing the setlist off of the stage with the neon green duct tape that had previously affixed it firmly to the floor intact.

I hastily backed off the stage the same way I crawled onto it, hoping no one would spot me and fearing some sort of retribution for my undoubtedly frowned upon behavior. Could I be banned for life from Great Scott or worse, from all Bowery Boston venues, for stealing a setlist? For my new lifestyle, this would have been a fate worse than death, and I was still too green to know the rules. Thankfully, to my surprise, no one seemed to care.

With my newfound loot, I was riding high. I withdrew some cash from the bar's ATM that had a sign above it which read *CASH ONLY: live within your means.* I had recently moved to Boston at age twenty-four, worked at a tech agency as a project manager, and started seeing multiple concerts each week—I most certainly was *not* living within my means at this moment. I purchased a PBR tallboy anyway (the drink of choice at this establishment) hoping to gain the liquid courage I needed to meet a "real" artist in the flesh for the first time.

Before long, my half-full "last call" beer was warm, but somehow, I struck up the nerve to talk to Liz Nistico, lead singer of HOLYCHILD, anyway. She was still dressed in what would be the *least* elaborate on-stage costume I'd end up seeing her wear: a sparkly silver pair of high-waisted leggings and a matching long-sleeve top with black feathery cuffs. She had perfectly placed rhinestone flowers down the middle part of her wavy short brown hair and a small black tattoo of a foreign symbol on her left side by her ribcage, nearly obscured by her crop top.

We posed for photos with each other and she signed Connor's copy of the setlist that he'd stolen from a more accessible part of the stage (one benefit of dancing in the front row). Liz wrote affectionately in the margins of his copy of the setlist, *Connor, SO nice to have you front row. You have the best energy. Until we meet again, XX Liz.* She thanked us for our willingness to dance and sing our hearts out to every song off of their recently released album, *The Shape of Brat Pop to Come*, and we complimented her and Louie on their performance.

Newly emboldened by my chat with Liz and determined to impress my new concert-going partner, I didn't think twice when Connor dared me to talk to the other band member and multi-instrumentalist, Louie Diller, who was in the middle of a conversation with two girls that he seemed to know personally. I jumped in to compliment his colorful oversized '80s-style windbreaker. His response was as warm and welcome as Liz's, and we chatted for a few minutes.

The next day, Connor and I were exchanging tweets with the band about how great it was to meet them the night before. Who was this new confident woman who took pictures with artists, crawled across stages for setlists, and got replies from bands on Twitter? Was this going to become the norm?

Yearning for more live music, we ended up at a free Atlas Genius and New Politics show on the Boston Common that afternoon. Music every day. This was the new norm, and I was finally in my element.

HOLYCHILD was the first somewhat famous band that I had ever met. I'd gone to my fair share of concerts, large and small, but never thought to hang around after the set to say hi to the bands. They were busy, famous, talented musicians, on a stage and behind a mic. I was just a lowly fan—happy to pay for my ticket, experience the music from afar, maybe buy a T-shirt, and then promptly exit the venue in a mass of impatient people who always seemingly expected that the speed at which they accessed their car would result in drastically differing levels of traffic exiting the venue (even though it never did).

On the other hand, Connor and his friends regularly met bands, stole setlists, got autographs, and heard back from musicians on social media. Meeting Connor had changed my life forever, and I was only getting a glimpse of it at the HOLYCHILD show.

Now, more than four years later and still attending several live shows a month, Connor and I are very much in love and we live together. I bet you didn't think this book was actually a love story disguised by a bunch of data in the middle, did you?

His HOLYCHILD setlist is still in the pristine condition in which he stole it, despite all of our adventures together—a messy roommate who smeared bright orange French dressing on everything, a move just around the corner in Southie from his two-bedroom apartment into my tiny room in a shared townhouse, across the country from Boston to Denver, and then back to Southie again.

My copy barely survived that night. I somehow ripped it straight down the middle into two pieces. Though it's redundant to have two copies in one seven-hundred-square-foot apartment, I still hold on to it dearly as an artifact from the night that I met a band for the first time after a show; from the night that I started to fall in love with Connor through experiencing live music with him.

APPENDIX

INTRODUCTION

Berklee Institute for Creative Entrepreneurship. "Fair Music: Transparency and Payment Flows in the Music Industry." Rethink Music. July 14, 2015. http://www.rethink-music.com/research.

Daily Beast. "Van Dyke Parks on How Songwriters Are Getting Screwed in the Digital Age." Updated July 12, 2017. https://www.thedailybeast.com/van-dyke-parks-on-how-songwriters-are-getting-screwed-in-the-digital-age.

Hunter, David. "Music Copyright in Britain to 1800." Music & Letters 67, no. 3 (1986): 269-82. www.jstor.org/stable/735889.

KIDinaKORNER Records. "Creators." Last accessed January 27, 2020. http://kidinakorner.com/creators.

The Manifesto. "Seth Kallen." Wisdom: A Portrait Series. Last accessed January 27, 2020. https://themanifesto.co/seth-kallen.

Miller, Larry. "How Music Got Modernized." October 24, 2018. In *Musonomics*. SoundCloud. Podcast, MP3 audio. https://soundcloud.com/musonomics/how-music-got-modernized.

Miller, Larry. "Mind the (Value) Gap." October 18, 2019. In *Musonomics*. SoundCloud. Podcast, MP3 audio. https://soundcloud.com/musonomics/mind-the-value-gap.

Rethink Music at Berklee College of Music. "Rethink Music Fair Music Workshop." October 2, 2015, video. https://vimeo.com/143443988.

Ross, Danny. "How To Manage Pop Stars Like X Ambassadors." *Forbes*, February 8, 2018. https://www.forbes.com/sites/dannyross1/2018/02/08/how-to-manage-pop-stars-like-x-ambassadors/#d0cc460137bf.

This Fiction Management. "Homepage." Last accessed January 27, 2020. http://www.thisfiction.com/.

US Department of Labor. "Changes in Basic Minimum Wages in Non-Farm Employment Under State Law: Selected Years 1968 to 2019." Wage and Hour Division. Revised January 2020. https://www.dol.gov/agencies/whd/state/minimum-wage/history.

Wikipedia. "X Ambassadors." Last accessed January 27, 2020. https://en.wikipedia.org/wiki/X_Ambassadors.

CHAPTER ONE

Kayata, Erin. "Last Winter's Snowmageddon, by the numbers." *The Boston Globe*, November 8, 2015, Examiner. https://www.bostonglobe.com/magazine/2015/11/08/last-winter-snowmageddon-numbers/RgkSKmB3nZJTXijQgRafYM/story.html.

Kidson, Frank. "Handel's Publisher, John Walsh, His Successors, and Contemporaries." *The Musical Quarterly* 6, no. 3 (1920): 430-50. www.jstor.org/stable/737971.

Krueger, Alan B. Rockonomics: *A Backstage Tour of What the Music Industry Can Teach Us about Economics and Life* (New York: Penguin Random House, 2019).

Lizzo. "8 years of touring, giving out free tix to my undersold shows, sleepless nights in my car, losing my dad & giving up on music, playing shows for free beer." Twitter, November 25, 2019, 1:29 a.m. https://twitter.com/lizzo/status/1198851244766269442.

Miller, Larry. "Mind the (Value) Gap." October 18, 2019. In *Musonomics*. SoundCloud. Podcast, MP3 audio. https://soundcloud.com/musonomics/mind-the-value-gap.

Recording Industry Association of America (RIAA). "US Recorded Music Revenues by Format." US Sales Database. Last accessed January 27, 2020. https://www.riaa.com/u-s-sales-database/.

CHAPTER TWO

Billboard. "Hot 100 Chart." Last accessed January 27, 2020. https://www.billboard.com/charts/hot-100.

Dana Point Rehab. "Demi Lovato Doing Well After Overdose and Drug Rehab." October 22, 2018. https://danapointrehabcampus.com/blog/2018/10/demi-lovato-doing-well-after-overdose-and-drug-r/.

Hardie, Richard. "All Fairly Engraven?": Punches in England, 1695 to 1706." *Notes* 61, no. 3 (2005): 617-33. www.jstor.org/stable/4487436.

Hunter, David. "Music Copyright in Britain to 1800." *Music & Letters* 67, no. 3 (1986): 269-82. www.jstor.org/stable/735889.

Hunter, David. "The Printing of Opera and Song Books in England, 1703-1726." *Notes* 46, no. 2 (1989): 328-51. doi:10.2307/941073.

Krause, Jason. "BREAKING UP DOWNLOADING: Recording Industry Keeps Fighting Illegal File Sharing With Even More Lawsuits." *ABA Journal* 92, no. 4 (2006): 16-18. www.jstor.org/stable/27846145.

Krueger, Alan B. Rockonomics: *A Backstage Tour of What the Music Industry Can Teach Us about Economics and Life* (New York: Penguin Random House, 2019).

Miller, Larry. "How Music Got Modernized." October 24, 2018. In *Musonomics*. SoundCloud. Podcast, MP3 audio. https://soundcloud.com/musonomics/how-music-got-modernized.

Miller, Larry. "Mind the (Value) Gap." October 18, 2019. In *Musonomics*. SoundCloud. Podcast, MP3 audio. https://soundcloud.com/musonomics/mind-the-value-gap.

"The Constitution of the United States: The Bill of Rights & All Amendments." Last accessed on January 27, 2020. https://constitutionus.com/.

Witt, Stephen. *How Music Got Free: A Story of Obsession and Invention* (New York: Penguin Books, 2016).

CHAPTER THREE

Bilis, Madeline. "The Best Time to Sign a New Lease in Boston Is During Winter." *Boston Magazine*, January 29, 2018. https://www.bostonmagazine.com/property/2018/01/29/best-time-new-lease-boston-winter/.

"Dave Matthews Band's 'Everyday' Turns A Page." *Billboard Magazine*, February 9, 2001. https://www.billboard.com/articles/news/80597/dave-matthews-bands-everyday-turns-a-page.

"Dave Matthews Band Revels In 'Busted Stuff.'" *Billboard Magazine*, June 7, 2002. https://www.billboard.com/articles/news/75488/dave-matthews-band-revels-in-busted-stuff.

DistroKid. "How Long Does It Take for My Album to Be Available in Stores?" Last accessed January 27, 2020. https://distrokid.zendesk.com/hc/en-us/articles/360013649293-How-Long-Does-It-Take-for-My-Album-to-Be-Available-in-Stores-.

Gokhman, Roman. "Q&A: MisterWives 'Bloom' Again with New Music and More on the Way." *Riff Magazine*, November 21, 2019. https://www.riffmagazine.com/qa/misterwives-bloom-again/.

Heller, Greg. "The Long, Botched Summer: The Birth, Death and Rebirth of a DMB Album." *Rolling Stone*, July 11, 2001. https://web.archive.org/web/20071001211510/http://www.rollingstone.com/news/story/5932312/the_long_botched_summer.

Honda Trinidad. "Honda Surprising Monsters Calling Home." September 25, 2012. YouTube Video, 00:35. https://www.youtube.com/watch?v=FmQfnMss-io.

Indigo Productions. "How Much Does It Cost to Make a Music Video." Video Production Blog. Posted on August 23, 2013. https://www.indigoprod.com/nyc-video-production-blog/2013/08/how-much-does-it-cost-to-make-a-music-video/.

Krueger, Alan B. *Rockonomics: A Backstage Tour of What the Music Industry Can Teach Us about Economics and Life* (New York: Penguin Random House, 2019).

Mosk, Mitch. "MisterWives' Unapologetic 'WhyWhyWhy' is a Dynamic Post-Breakup Reckoning." *Atwood Magazine*, August 1, 2019. https://atwoodmagazine.com/mwww-whywhywhy-misterwives-song-review/.

Recording Industry Association of America (RIAA). "US Recorded Music Revenues by Format." US Sales Database. Last accessed January 27, 2020. https://www.riaa.com/u-s-sales-database/.

Ross, Danny. "How To Be a Hit Music Producer with a $2,000 Budget." *Forbes*, September 21, 2018. https://www.forbes.com/sites/dannyross1/2018/09/21/how-to-be-a-hit-music-producer-with-a-2000-budget/#1715e25d2b22.

Spotify for Artists. "How Do I Get My Music On a Spotify Playlist? Submit Music for Playlist Consideration." FAQ. Last accessed

January 27, 2020. https://artists.spotify.com/faq/promotion#how-do-i-submit-music-to-your-editorial-team.

Spotify for Artists. "Provider Directory." Accessed January 27, 2020. https://artists.spotify.com/directory/distribution.

Stebbins, Samuel, and Evan Comen. "America's 24 dying industries include sound studios, textiles, newspapers." *USA Today*, updated January 4, 2018, Economy. https://www.usatoday.com/story/money/economy/2017/12/28/americas-25-dying-industries-include-sound-studios-textiles-newspapers/982514001/.

Witt, Stephen. *How Music Got Free: A Story of Obsession and Invention* (New York: Penguin Books, 2016).

CHAPTER FOUR

Andrews, Travis M. "Can Taylor Swift Really Rerecord Her Entire Music Catalogue?" *The Washington Post*, August 22, 2019, Pop Culture. https://www.washingtonpost.com/arts-entertainment/2019/08/22/can-taylor-swift-really-rerecord-her-entire-music-catalogue/.

Conte, Jack. "Pomplamoose 2014 Tour Profits." Medium, November 24, 2014. https://medium.com/@jackconte/pomplamoose-2014-tour-profits-67435851ba37.

Coscarelli, Joe. "Taylor Swift Announces New Record Deal With Universal Music." *The New York Times*, November 19, 2018. https://www.nytimes.com/2018/11/19/arts/music/taylor-swift-record-deal-universal-republic.html.

Coscarelli, Joe. "Taylor Swift Says She Will Rerecord Her Old Music. Here's How." *The New York Times*, updated August 27, 2019. https://www.nytimes.com/2019/08/22/arts/music/taylor-swift-rerecord-albums.html.

Huang, Chun-Yao. "File Sharing as a Form of Music Consumption." *International Journal of Electronic Commerce* 9, no. 4 (2005): 37-55. www.jstor.org/stable/27751164.

Krueger, Alan B. *Rockonomics: A Backstage Tour of What the Music Industry Can Teach Us about Economics and Life* (New York: Penguin Random House, 2019).

Leviatan, Yoni. "Making Music: The 6 Stages of Music Production." Waves Audio. Blog. July 27, 2017. https://www.waves.com/six-stages-of-music-production.

Mandell, Josh. "Where Does Live Nation Have Room To Grow?" *Forbes*, March 4, 2019. https://www.forbes.com/sites/joshmandell/2019/03/04/where-does-live-nation-have-room-to-grow/#33626f0116de.

McCafferty, Kelly. "Real Songs, Real Talk, and Real People: A Conversation with MisterWives." *Atwood Magazine*, October 28, 2019. https://atwoodmagazine.com/mw19-misterwives-interview-2019-music/.

NYU Steinhardt. "Larry Miller: Clinical Music Associate Professor and Director, Music Business Program." Last accessed January 27, 2020. https://steinhardt.nyu.edu/people/larry-miller.

Outerloop Group. "What Is the Difference Between the Producer, Engineer, and Mixer?" February 19, 2019. YouTube Video. https://www.youtube.com/watch?v=v8qHEr9UX4E.

Passman, Donald S. *All You Need to Know About the Music Business Ninth Edition* (Simon and Schuster, 2015). Kindle.

Resnikoff, Paul. "Two-Thirds of All Music Sold Comes from Just 3 Companies." Digital Music News, August 3, 2015. https://www.digitalmusicnews.com/2016/08/03/two-thirds-music-sales-come-three-major-labels/.

Sisario, Ben and Joe Coscarelli. "Taylor Swift's Feud With Scooter Braun Spotlights Musicians' Struggles to Own Their Work." *The New York Times*, July 1, 2019. https://www.nytimes.

com/2019/07/01/arts/music/taylor-swift-master-recordings.html.

CHAPTER FIVE

GroundUp Music. "About." Last accessed January 27, 2020. https://groundupmusic.net/about.

LinkedIn. "Becky Blumenthal." Last accessed January 27, 2020. https://www.linkedin.com/in/beckyblumenthal/.

Miller, Larry. "Mind the (Value) Gap." October 18, 2019. In *Musonomics*. SoundCloud. Podcast, MP3 audio. https://soundcloud.com/musonomics/mind-the-value-gap.

Ross, Danny. "How to Manage Pop Stars Like X Ambassadors." *Forbes*, February 8, 2018. https://www.forbes.com/sites/dannyross1/2018/02/08/how-to-manage-pop-stars-like-x-ambassadors/#d0cc460137bf.

StageRight. "An Interview with Tour Manager Chris Walkowski." July 10, 2019. https://performance.stageright.com/blog/tour-manager-interview-chris-walkowski/.

CHAPTER SIX

Angelakos, Michael. "it's the 5th-anniversary of Gossamer, an album that is about and the product of a manic episode. I nearly lost everything, including my life." Twitter, July 23, 2017, 10:28 p.m. https://twitter.com/passionpit/status/889311323389079552.

Berklee Institute for Creative Entrepreneurship. "Fair Music: Transparency and Payment Flows in the Music Industry." Rethink Music. July 14, 2015. http://www.rethink-music.com/research.

Byrne, David. "Open the Music Industry's Black Box." *The New York Times*, July 31, 2015, Opinion. https://www.nytimes.

com/2015/08/02/opinion/sunday/open-the-music-industrys-black-box.html.

Conte, Jack. "Pomplamoose 2014 Tour Profits." Medium, November 24, 2014. https://medium.com/@jackconte/pomplamoose-2014-tour-profits-67435851ba37.

Coscarelli, Joe. "Taylor Swift Announces New Record Deal With Universal Music." *The New York Times*, November 19, 2018. https://www.nytimes.com/2018/11/19/arts/music/taylor-swift-record-deal-universal-republic.html.

Daily Beast. "Van Dyke Parks on How Songwriters Are Getting Screwed in the Digital Age." Updated July 12, 2017. https://www.thedailybeast.com/van-dyke-parks-on-how-songwriters-are-getting-screwed-in-the-digital-age.

Forde, Eamonn. "Where Concert Ticket Money Goes: Who's Getting Rich Off Of Live Music's Golden Age?" *The Guardian*, January 30, 2017, Music. https://www.theguardian.com/music/2017/jan/30/where-does-concert-ticket-money-go.

Ganz, Jacob. "The Concert Ticket Food Chain: Where Your Money Goes." *NPR News*, April 6, 2011, The Record. https://www.npr.org/sections/therecord/2011/04/07/134851302/the-concert-ticket-food-chain-where-your-money-goes.

Kaplan, Ilana. "Passion Pit's Michael Angelakos on speaking out on mental health: 'People just want me to shut up and make music.'" *The Independent*, January 11, 2018. https://www.independent.co.uk/arts-entertainment/music/features/passion-pit-michael-angelakos-mental-health-make-music-wishart-group-a8152141.html.

Krueger, Alan B. *Rockonomics: A Backstage Tour of What the Music Industry Can Teach Us about Economics and Life* (New York: Penguin Random House, 2019).

Miller, Larry. "The Headwinds Facing Music Startups." June 7, 2016. In *Musonomics*. SoundCloud. Podcast, MP3 audio. https://

soundcloud.com/musonomics/the-headwinds-facing-music-startups.

Miller, Larry. "Mind the (Value) Gap." October 18, 2019. In *Musonomics*. SoundCloud. Podcast, MP3 audio. https://soundcloud.com/musonomics/mind-the-value-gap.

Miller, Larry. "The Transparency Moment." September 2, 2015. In *Musonomics*. SoundCloud. Podcast, MP3 audio. https://soundcloud.com/musonomics/the-transparency-moment.

Minsker, Evan and Matthew Strauss. "Passion Pit's Michael Angelakos Not Done With Music, but Says the Industry 'Nearly Killed' Him." *Pitchfork Magazine*, July 24, 2017. https://pitchfork.com/news/passion-pits-michael-angelakos-not-done-with-music-but-says-the-industry-nearly-killed-him/.

Ross, Danny. "How to Manage Pop Stars Like X Ambassadors." *Forbes*, February 8, 2018. https://www.forbes.com/sites/dannyross1/2018/02/08/how-to-manage-pop-stars-like-x-ambassadors/#d0cc460137bf.

Spotify for Artists. "How Spotify Pays Artists." November 15, 2018. Video. https://artists.spotify.com/videos/the-game-plan/how-spotify-pays-you.

Team Jukely. "Where Does Your Money Go When You Buy a Concert Ticket?" Jukely. April 30, 2018. https://www.fouroverfour.jukely.com/culture/where-does-money-go-concert-ticket/.

Thomson, Kristin. "Music and How the Money Flows." Future of Music Coalition. Updated March 10, 2015. https://futureofmusic.org/article/article/music-and-how-money-flows.

The Trichordist. "2018 Streaming Price Bible! Per Stream Rates Drop as Streaming Volume Grows. YouTube's Value Gap is Very Real." January 29, 2018. https://thetrichordist.com/2019/01/29/2018-streaming-price-bible-per-stream-rates-drop-as-streaming-volume-grows-youtubes-value-gap-is-very-real/.

Recording Industry Association of America (RIAA). "US Recorded Music Revenues by Format." US Sales Database. Last accessed January 27, 2020. https://www.riaa.com/u-s-sales-database/.

Spotify Group. "Spotify: DREAMDIVE." DREAMDIVE Artist Profile. Spotify. Version 1.1.26.501.gbe11e53b (2020). https://open.spotify.com/artist/3zVDD7fyvcLYxW22ZaVvgu?si=26yqxAS_TmuxEFzZ3ZIUoQ.

CHAPTER SEVEN

Coscarelli, Joe. "Taylor Swift Says She Will Rerecord Her Old Music. Here's How." *The New York Times*, updated August 27, 2019. https://www.nytimes.com/2019/08/22/arts/music/taylor-swift-rerecord-albums.html.

Greene, Jayson. "Chance the Rapper 'No Problem' [ft. 2 Chainz and Lil Wayne]." *Pitchfork Magazine*, May 13, 2016. https://pitchfork.com/reviews/tracks/18269-chance-the-rapper-no-problem-ft-2-chainz-and-lil-wayne/.

Krueger, Alan B. *Rockonomics: A Backstage Tour of What the Music Industry Can Teach Us about Economics and Life* (New York: Penguin Random House, 2019).

Lockett, Dee. "Did Chance the Rapper Just Save SoundCloud?" *Vulture*, July 14, 2017. https://www.vulture.com/2017/07/chance-the-rapper-soundcloud.html.

Miller, Larry. "How Music Got Modernized." October 24, 2018. In *Musonomics*. SoundCloud. Podcast, MP3 audio. https://soundcloud.com/musonomics/how-music-got-modernized.

Sofar Sounds. "Homepage." Last accessed January 27, 2020. https://www.sofarsounds.com/.

Swift, Taylor. *Don't know what else to do*. Twitter, November 14, 2019, 6:35 p.m. Photo.

Swift, Taylor. "Taylor Swift—Live at the 2019 American Music Awards." November 26, 2019. YouTube Video, 00:40. https://www.youtube.com/watch?v=SVY8I46dkb0.

Wang, Amy X. "Why Chance the Rapper—Who Just Made Grammy History—Gives His Music Away for Free." Quartz, February 13, 2017. https://qz.com/908815/why-chance-the-rapper-who-just-made-grammy-history-gives-his-music-away-for-free/.

CHAPTER EIGHT

Bottom of the Hill. "Booking." Last accessed January 27, 2020. http://www.bottomofthehill.com/booking.html.

Evans, Matt. Email message to author. March 13, 2019.

hello, witchsong. "Send Me Your Magic: Paperwhite Live in DC." Medium. June 2, 2016. https://medium.com/witchsong/send-me-your-magic-paperwhite-live-in-dc-9b0e1f47a4e8.

Indie On The Move. "About." Last accessed January 27, 2020. https://www.indieonthemove.com/about.

Miller, Larry. "The Transparency Moment." September 2, 2015. In *Musonomics*. SoundCloud. Podcast, MP3 audio. https://soundcloud.com/musonomics/the-transparency-moment.

www.ingramcontent.com/pod-product-compliance
Lightning Source LLC
LaVergne TN
LVHW011833060526
838200LV00053B/4003